A Parent's Guide to Common and Uncommon School Problems

by:
David A. Gross, M.D.
and
Irl L. Extein, M.D.

T·H·E
PIA
PRESS

This book is not intended to replace personal medical care and supervision; there is no substitute for the experience and information that a doctor can provide.

Proper medical care should always be tailored to the individual patient. If you read something in this book that seems to conflict with your doctor's instructions, contact your doctor. Your doctor may have medically sound reasons for prescribing medication in a manner that may differ from the information presented in this book.

Also note that this book may not contain every drug or brand of drug currently prescribed in the treatment of child and adolescent psychiatric conditions.

If you have any questions about any medicine or treatment in this book, consult your doctor or pharmacist.

In addition, the patient names and cases used do not represent actual people, but are composite cases drawn from several sources.

We gratefully acknowledge the following for the right to reprint or adapt published material:

"The Homework Problem Checklist" from pp 46–48 of Levine, FM, and Anesko, KM. *Winning the Homework War.* Englewood Cliffs, NJ: Prentice Hall, 1987.

"Roadblocks to Communication" from pp 32–33 of Gordon, T. *P.E.T. In Action.* New York: Bantam Books, 1976.

"Parent-Teacher Conference" from pp 245–246 of Rich, D. *MegaSkills.* Boston: Houghton Mifflin Company, 1988.

Dedication

To our parents, who raised us with concern, involvement, and understanding; to our own delightful children—Sam and Shari; Melissa, Jason, Andrew, and Seth—from whose development we continue to learn; and to our wives and parenting partners, Myrna and Barbara.

ACKNOWLEDGMENTS

We gratefully acknowledge the assistance and cooperation of our colleagues, staff, and patients of Fair Oaks Hospital, particularly the Children's Adolescent Unit.

In addition, we are especially thankful for the considerable contributions of Margot Embree Fisher to the creation of this manuscript, and to James Cayea for his assistance.

CONTENTS

INTRODUCTION

WITH ALL the child care books on the market today, who would blame parents for thinking that they needed to be experts in order to raise a happy, well-adjusted child? That is simply not true, or, as an old friend of ours used to say, "You don't have to write a cookbook, to know how to cook." The same saying applies to parenting: after all, there were good parents long before there were experts. All you need to be a good parent—besides love and concern for your child—is clear thinking and common sense.

We know this firsthand, because both of us are parents as well as psychiatrists. In medical school, we learned the importance of *listening* and *communicating*. We were taught to listen to our patients' hearts and lungs for any unusual sounds that might indicate a medical disorder, and we were taught to listen to what our patients said—and did not say—to discern clues that might reveal the patient's mental or physical state. A hesitant answer to a physician's question, a downward glance of the eyes, or shrug of the shoulders might indicate that there was an underlying problem. But effective communication is more than listening. As physicians, we must be able to explain medical conditions and treatments clearly to the patient. Patients who do not understand either their condition or treatment will not usually remain patients for long.

Unfortunately, as the emphasis on medical technology grows, this old-fashioned physician-patient communication is frequently ignored. Like the physician-patient dialogue, parent-child and parent-teacher communication is usually the best, and most often overlooked, means of determining your child's school problem.

Our practical experience as parents has proven the value of this advice. The single most important element in good parenting is effective communication.

Sounds simple, doesn't it? In some ways it is: Anyone can learn to communicate effectively. Still, as you will learn from reading this book, effective communication takes patience and practice. Once you master it, you will find that you can prevent minor school problems from becoming major ones, and help the child with major problems get back on track.

In this book, we share some of the many stories we've heard from our patients over the years. Naturally, we've changed names and identifying details to protect our patients' privacy. We also reveal some of our personal experiences as parents dealing with our own children's school problems.

Although we may occasionally complain about our kids, most of us know that parenting is usually a very positive, if challenging, experience. Still, there are times of trouble and crisis, and these often involve our children's schools.

Why focus on school problems? Well, for one thing, once they reach school age, our children spend more time in school than they do at home. And it is school, with its social stresses and pressure to perform, that often brings children's problems to the surface. Here are some examples of various kinds of school problems—do any of these stories sound familiar?

James* puts up such a fuss every morning when he is dropped off at kindergarten that his mother has been late to work four times this week.

Although Benjamin has always been what his parents

---

*NOTE: Throughout this book, patient names have been changed and identities disguised to protect privacy. In addition, we use the pronoun "he" instead of relying on the cumbersome "he/she." Although some problems are more common in boys and others more common in girls, the pronoun used is not meant to suggest that only one sex or the other is vulnerable to a particular problem.

call "a good kid," his second-grade teacher complains that he bullies the other children.

A year after his family moved, Larry—once a seemingly outgoing, rambunctious fifth-grader—mysteriously can't seem to make friends.

Thirteen-year-old Chris constantly gets into trouble. In his latest escapade, he was caught cutting class.

Felicia, who used to get straight A's and B's, just brought home a report card with three D's and an F.

These kids, like most children with school problems, are feeling unhappy, frustrated, and out of control. Their parents are unhappy because they, too, feel helpless. The purpose of this book is to guide you and your child through these troubled times. Some of the questions we will answer are:

- What can you do when your child has problems at school?
- How can you tell if a problem is serious or just a "phase" the child will outgrow?
- How can you keep relatively minor school problems from becoming major ones?
- How can problem behavior be corrected?
- When does your child need professional help?

Obviously, not every school problem is a major problem. The goal of this book is to give parents the information they need to put school problems into perspective and to prevent problems from arising. In addition, we discuss how parents can tell when a problem really is a problem. And, perhaps most important, we give parents the tools they need to deal with their problems effectively. Armed with the proper perspective and the proper tools—and a sense of humor—parents can actually appreciate this most important aspect of their child's development.

Read on to find the answers to your child's school problems . . .

CHAPTER 1

PUT THE PROBLEM IN PERSPECTIVE

RECENTLY, a highly respected colleague of ours told us a personal story that illustrates just how difficult it is to keep your child's problems in perspective:

Last month, my mother complained that my 9-month-old son cried violently every time she tried to take the child away from my wife. After repeatedly failing to quiet the boy, my mother snidely remarked, "Your *brother's* child *never* cried when I picked *him* up!" The implication was clear: There was something wrong with my child and it was probably my fault. I began to wonder what was wrong with my son, and if there was something wrong I was doing. Well, even though I'm a psychiatrist and should definitely know better, it took me three days to realize that my son's reaction was a normal separation anxiety response for his age—he should have cried! My brother's son had reacted abnormally, not mine. I only wish I had realized this while my mother was still visiting.

This story illustrates just how difficult it is to keep the proper perspective. Even a trained psychiatrist fell into the trap of not understanding normal development—of actually feeling guilty for his son's normal reaction. However, rather than continuing to feel guilty for his child's very normal reaction, the psychiatrist had the knowledge—eventually—to understand the appropriateness of his child's behavior. It is this knowledge that we would like to share with you in this chapter.

WHAT'S NORMAL? AND WHAT'S NOT?

To understand and deal with your child's problem behavior, you also have to know what constitutes "normal" behavior. Children's behavior and learning patterns have been studied intensively by psychiatrists, psychologists, and social scientists interested in how children grow and develop. In particular, we must acknowledge the excellent work of David Elkind, Haim Ginott, Jean Piaget, and Erik Erikson for their outstanding contributions to our knowledge of child development. Their work has had great influence on our thinking.

Altogether, researchers have studied thousands of children from many different countries and cultures. One of the most interesting things they've found is that all children—no matter what country or culture—go through four major developmental stages: infancy, early childhood, childhood, and adolescence.

Well, of course, you're probably thinking. Everyone knows that kids go through different stages. But it is not as simple as it seems. At each stage, the child develops specific, well-defined intellectual, social, and emotional skills. In other words, growing up is more than just a process of physical maturation, and it is more than just learning new information. As children grow, the *way* in which they learn changes, and this in turns lets them learn new kinds of information.

Children do not—and cannot—think and reason like adults. The mental abilities needed to reason and think and judge and make decisions like an adult are developed in stages. In the same way, different emotional and social skills are learned at different ages. These emotional and social skills are just as important to a child's success in school as mental skills.

It is important to recognize the limitations of each age group. Pushing a child too fast—setting unrealistic goals—will only lead to frustration and disappointment for both you and the child.

Here is a summary of the kinds of achievement, or developmental milestones, that characterize the different stages.

STAGE I: BIRTH TO TWO YEARS

There are three major emotional, intellectual, and social developments in this stage.

Emotional/Psychological

The very first of these is bonding, or emotional attachment, to the mother. This is critical to the child's learning and development, because it motivates him to learn and explore. The reverse side of the baby's bonding is that he becomes afraid of being separated from his mother. As we saw in the anecdote that began this chapter, it is not unusual for a newborn baby to cry when picked up by anyone but his mother. Of course, this fear of separation is a healthy, self-protective instinct for an infant. But as we will see, it can also be the source of problems in an older child.

Intellectual

The primary intellectual development of this stage is seen in the child's exploration of his world, as he gets to know the objects around him. The baby learns about his world through physical exploration—feeling and throwing and dropping things, and putting as many of them into his mouth as allowed! He also learns to talk. By two years, the child has learned most of the words that describe the objects in his everyday world, and he speaks well enough to let you know about most of his needs and desires.

Social

Socially, this is when the child learns to trust people and the world in general. This is an important counterbalance to attachment to the mother. If a baby's basic needs are met consistently and reliably, he will develop a sense of trust, an understanding that the world and the people in it are essentially good. But a baby who is neglected and ignored, or who gets only sporadic attention, will not become trustful. Instead, he will feel that the world is unfriendly and unpredictable, and he will withdraw.

Without a basic feeling of trust, children cannot grow emotionally and socially—and they won't be inspired to learn.

STAGE II: TWO TO SIX YEARS

In the next stage, early childhood, the child's abilities flower. Physical changes are obvious, and the child becomes much more coordinated. As he develops, he learns new ways of thinking and understanding the world and people around him, allowing him to use more complicated language.

Intellectual

After two years, children learn that an object—say, Uncle Fred's cocker spaniel—can be symbolized by a picture or even by words, even though the dog is not actually there. They learn to reason: "If I pull the doggie's tail, he'll try to bite me." This is the stage when children start to express mental discoveries with language, and they learn to express anxiety and fears in dreams and symbolic play. For example, in the car on the way to visit Uncle Fred and his skittish cocker spaniel, the child may play with his stuffed dog, pulling its tail and pretending that it is biting him.

Social

For most children, this is the stage when they begin to form relationships with people outside the immediate family. This includes other adult caretakers, such as babysitters and day care teachers, as well as children their own age in playgroups or around the neighborhood. Many families throughout the country have found participation in organized "Mommy and Me" play groups to be especially helpful in fostering social development in this stage.

Emotional/Psychological

At this stage, children start to realize that they are relatively small and powerless, which explains their fascination with giant animals like dinosaurs and with cartoon superheroes. They also start to realize that their parents are not as perfect and powerful as they believed when they were toddlers.

In Stage II, children are at a crossroads. They have a natural sense of curiosity and an interest in exploration, and your reactions will either encourage them to learn new things and make new friends, or to be timid and withdrawn. This is the age when children ask endless "why" questions—sometimes, it seem, just to see how you will react. They are also constantly getting into things, taking them apart and trying to put them back together again.

You can stimulate this growth by giving the child the proper challenges, but some parents push too hard at this point. If you expect too much from your child—for example, starting toilet training before the child is ready, or pushing a three-year-old to read—you're setting the child up for failure. Maintaining a balance between enough stimulation and unrealistic expectations prepares the child to succeed, not fail, when he enters school. You also must create an atmosphere of love and security in the home that encourages your child to learn and to develop friendships.

STAGE III: SEVEN TO ELEVEN YEARS

During these early school years, the child builds on and develops the skills learned in Stage II.

Intellectual

In this stage, the child's reading and arithmetic skills are enhanced, and he begins to understand fairly complicated material. He is also able to learn rules, especially in reading, arithmetic, and sports. Children this age often make up their own games and rules, which helps them stretch and improve their new skills.

Social

Like the intellectual skills of this stage, the child's social skills also become more sophisticated. He becomes more independent and separate from his parents. At the same time, other adults (such as teachers, coaches, neighbors, and relatives) become more important to the child. He also gets more attached to friends his own age. In fact, he will probably have a circle of friends as well as a "best friend."

Emotional/Psychological

The most important psychological development of this stage is that the child now develops an image of himself as either able to succeed or doomed to fail. If the home atmosphere is caring and supportive, the child will be able to weather the storms of occasional setbacks at school. But if all he hears at home is that he is stupid and lazy, then problems with schoolwork will only be reinforced.

STAGE IV: TWELVE AND OLDER

The rapid and dramatic physical changes of adolescence are obvious—so much so that they can cover up even more dramatic shifts in the child's thinking and view of the world.

Intellectual

Again, there's a change in the *way* a child thinks, for in this stage, he learns to reason like an adult. The child can start to master complicated concepts. Schoolwork may include sophisticated subjects such as literary criticism, political science, advanced mathematics and science, and even philosophy.

Social

Socially, adolescence is an uncertain and changeable time; this is the final transition to adulthood. Teens are struggling to form and project an identity as they become more independent from their parents. Kids who were best friends in grade school may drift apart in high school as they identify themselves with different crowds. Teens also discover their sexual identity, and usually start dating. And as they assert their independence, they often discover the principle of parental imperfection. In your child's infancy, you were perfect and all-powerful. As he got older, he found out that you had certain limitations. But now that he is in his teens, everything you do is wrong—from the clothes you wear, to the music you listen to, and to the politics you support. But when he is in his twenties, he will probably discover that you're okay again.

Emotional/Psychological

Teenagers are notoriously moody; their moods can swing from one end of the emotional spectrum to another with dizzying speed. Try to keep this in mind during the times when your teen is criticizing you or claiming that everything in his life is messed up and the world is a miserable place. Things may not look so bleak in a few hours, especially if he gets a phone call from the girl he asked out last weekend.

This does not mean you should ignore serious disturbances in a teen's mood and behavior. So much has been said about adolescence being a time of trouble and turmoil that many people think that problems are inevitable. That just isn't true, and an unhappy, out-of-control teenager needs your help just as much as a six-year-old does. This is the age when kids are at the most risk of getting into serious trouble: with sex, with drug and alcohol abuse, and with the law. Keep the channels of communication open, and watch for signs that your child is in over his head; you owe it to him. Otherwise, small problems may escalate into big ones. An unwanted pregnancy, drug addiction, or dropping out of school can easily sentence the teenager to a lifetime of struggle.

WHAT CAN GO WRONG—AND WHEN

Looking at the different stages of development, you can see how important each stage is to the next. Growing up can be very complicated. It involves physical, emotional, and intellectual changes, and problems can develop at any stage for any number of reasons. The child may be in a stressful situation (such as having moved recently) or given tasks that aren't right for his developmental stage (such as having to take care of younger siblings). He may not have adjusted well to a previous stage. Or he may have a physical or medical problem, such as a learning disability, that interferes with his ability to adjust.

Since we're primarily concerned with school-age children in this book, we've divided the stages of development into three general categories:

The Early Years: Kindergarten to Third Grade (5/6 to 8/9 years)
The Middle Years: Fourth to Seventh Grade (9/10 to 12/13 years)
The Teens: Eighth to Twelfth Grade (13/14 to 17/18 years)

In the chart that follows, we've listed some of the typical problems that crop up at different ages. As the child grows up, the types of problems tend to change, because the challenges the child faces change. Also, the influence of peer pressure gets stronger and stronger as the child gets older. Keep in mind, though, that problems don't always occur in this order, and they don't occur only at certain ages. You may have a 5-year-old who disrupts kindergarten with his clownish antics, or a third-grader who won't communicate. This chart is just a general guide.

AGE	GRADE	TYPICAL PROBLEMS
The Early Years	Kindergarten to 3rd grade	Separation anxiety
		Hyperactivity
		Bullying
		Coordination difficulties
The Middle Years	4th to 7th grade	Homework hassles
		Class clown
		Lack of communication
		Poor grades
The Teens	8th grade to 12th grade	Truancy
		Depression
		Sex, drugs & rock'n roll
		Delinquency and
		cars, crime, charge cards
		Independence/dependence

Not every child will have problems in all of these areas, but just about every child will experience some kind of trouble sometime. When problems are minor, they are simply responses to the normal process of adjustment and maturation. In those cases, your concern and nonjudgmental guidance may be all the help your child needs. When problems are more serious, you—and your child—may need help from a teacher, school psychologist, psychiatrist, or some other professional.

Use your common sense and good judgment to separate "normal" adjustment from "abnormal" acting out. By using the effective communication skills we talk about in the next chapter, you will be able to determine the cause of the problem, and whether you need to enlist outside help.

THE STRESS CONNECTION

Earlier, we mentioned that problems can develop when children are placed in stressful situations. It may seen strange to think about children experiencing stress, since most people think of stress as an adult problem; childhood is supposed to be happy and carefree. Unfortunately, this wishful vision isn't always true.

Children, especially in our demanding modern society, are also subjected to stress—it just takes different forms (see the child stress symptoms in Chapter Six). There may be stressful situations at home or at school. The child may have a physical or medical problem that makes it hard to adjust at school. Or maybe the child is expected to do work that he is not ready for yet. Some of the stress of childhood can be avoided, but not all. Still, stress doesn't always have to lead to problems.

THE MIND-BRAIN-BODY CONNECTION

One of the most exciting areas of modern scientific research is a field called psychobiology. This new medical specialty is concerned with essential questions about human behavior: Why do we act the way we do? Why and how does mental illness develop? How does the chemistry of our bodies and brains affect our minds and our moods?

Although we don't have all the answers yet, we do know that even relatively small disturbances of the chemical balances in our bodies can be associated with serious emotional and mental problems. Disorders as different as autism, schizophrenia, depression, and panic attacks may all have a biological basis. There is also evidence that certain childhood problems, such as hyperactivity and separation anxiety, may be linked to abnormalities in body chemistry.

It is important that parents, teachers, and pediatricians be aware of the role that biological issues can play in a child's school problems. Any child who has repeated behavioral problems, or has trouble learning material that other children in the class have mastered, or who can't control his temper or energy level should have a thorough medical and psychological evaluation. Most of these conditions can be treated, but the success of treatment may depend on how early the problem is recognized.

WHEN EXPERT HELP IS NECESSARY

Most childhood problems are related to the normal stages of growing up. You yourself probably remember that many of your childhood troubles were dismissed by adults who said, "It's just a stage. You'll grow out of it." Chances are, you've said this to your own child on more than one occasion.

But persistent, extreme problems should never be ignored.

The following section provides descriptions of some of the disorders that are seen in school-age children. Learning disabilities are described first, followed by Attention-Deficit Hyperactivity Disorder, and then some of the other disorders that can contribute to school problems or require special education programs. This is not a complete listing, just a general outline. If your child exhibits symptoms of *any* of the conditions listed below, bring it to the immediate attention of the child's teacher, school counselor, or pediatrician—or all three.

LEARNING DISABILITY (LD)

Learning disability (LD) refers to a learning problem in a particular area, such as reading or arithmetic. Children with LD do not have problems learning in *all* areas. LD does not refer to children who do not learn because they don't work or haven't been taught properly. Nor does having a disability mean that the child is below average intelligence; in fact, many LD children have average or above average intelligence. A particular disability is thought to result from subtle changes in neurological functioning—in the way the brain processes information.

There are a wide range of learning disabilities that can affect achievement in reading, writing, and arithmetic. Most children with learning disorders can be helped if the condition is recognized early and if they are given adequate remedial support. Of course, there may be limitations to how much can be achieved, so you must set realistic goals.

Dyslexia

This is a catch-all term, referring to LD in general, or to the specific symptoms of word confusion or reversal of letters. Sometimes, a child has a similar problem with numbers. Most children can compensate for dyslexia, but early diagnosis and placement in a remedial program is critical. Otherwise, the child falls behind his peers and gets caught in a web of frustration, failure, and low self-esteem. Dyslexia may have a physical cause, which is why some physicians recommend drug therapy combined with other treatment approaches.

Communication Disorders

These are speech and language problems, ranging from stuttering to difficulties in pronunciation.

Mental Retardation

Unlike children with learning disorders, mentally retarded children have intellectual abilities significantly below average. They also have difficulty with normal social behavior.

Hearing Impairment

Even mild hearing loss can hinder learning in the usual classroom environment.

Visual Impairment

As with hearing, even slight vision problems can making learning difficult.

ATTENTION-DEFICIT HYPERACTIVITY DISORDER

All parents struggle at one time or another either to get their children's attention or to get them to comply with requests. Sometimes you may even feel like setting off an air-raid siren just to get your child to look away from the TV set. All children are somewhat distractable. But with *some* children, difficulty in paying attention is a more serious problem, interfering with their lives, especially at school, and often requiring treatment. These children usually have accompanying hyperactivity.

This combination is referred to by professionals as Attention-deficit Hyperactivity Disorder, or ADHD. But beware: the word *hyperactivity*, like the word *dyslexia*, is frequently misused. There are also many myths and misconceptions about this disorder. Hyperactivity, or ADHD, can interfere with learning, but it should not be confused with other learning disabilities. Most learning disabilities, such as dyslexia, result in failure to learn in a specific area. For example, the child may be fine at arithmetic but have trouble with spelling or writing.

ADHD is different. Instead of influencing only one learning skill, it can lead to a more general disorder, affecting attention span, concentration, and storage of information. In addition to having trouble sitting still and concentrating in class, children with ADHD generally have other behavioral problems. Their disruptive, impulsive, and aggressive behavior can lead to rejection by other children as well as problems with adults. Children with ADHD often develop a negative self-image, which can lead to many related problems.

Diagnosis

Diagnosis of ADHD is often made when a child is in first grade, where he is expected to be able to sit still and participate in structured activities. However, it may not be recognized until around third grade, when the child shows signs of reading problems. Also, at this age, teachers (and other children) tend to be less tolerant of the hyperactive child's daydreaming, fidgeting, restlessness, or aggressive behavior. Sometimes, the problem is not diagnosed until junior high. At this point, the problems have probably become severe.

Treatment

The good news about hyperactivity is that effective treatment is available. Stimulant medications are often effective in improving attention span, behavior, and school performance. In many cases, medication is augmented by a program of psychological and educational help. These medications don't "sedate" the child or cover up symptoms, as many people believe. Instead, they correct a biochemical imbalance in the brain, which allows the child to focus his attention and regulate his energy level normally. The medications usually should be combined with remedial education programs. It is critical to recognize the condition early: if left untreated, the child will fall further and further behind, until it becomes impossible for him to catch up with his classmates. He will also develop a poor-self image from years of failure, frustration, and social rejection.

Diet

There are several books on the market that recommend special additive-free, caffeine-free, and sugar-free diets to control hyperactivity. Unfortunately, there is no good scientific evidence that these expensive (and inconvenient) diets help significantly.

OTHER BEHAVIORAL-EMOTIONAL-PHYSICAL DISORDERS

Conduct Disorders

These are the serious behavioral problems commonly described as "delinquency." Children who get involved in criminal or violent acts should be treated by a specialist.

Age-Inappropriate Problems

As the name suggests, these problems involve behavior that might be somewhat troubling at one age, but is clearly alarming at another. For example, we wouldn't be horrified by a 13-year-old sneaking cigarettes or a 16-year-old having sex. But if a 6-year-old steals your cigarettes, or a 12-year-old is sexually active, the child probably has a serious emotional disorder requiring psychiatric attention.

Oppositional Defiant Disorder

A certain amount of defiance and disobedience is a normal aspect of growing up and becoming an independent adult. But persistent, extreme defiance is a sign of a deeper problem. Successful treatment usually includes the parents, who may need to modify the way they discipline the child.

Episodic and Organic Behavior Disorders

In these conditions, the child has outbursts of aggressive, disordered behavior, even though he may be calm and peaceful at other times. This kind of episodic or unpredictable loss of control may the sign of an underlying organic mental or brain disorder. Any child with such symptoms should have a thorough physical and mental examination.

Drug and Alcohol Dependency

Drug and alcohol abuse is more common among teenagers and younger children that most adults like to admit, and the consequences can be tragic. Learn to recognize the signs of drug and alcohol abuse (see Chapter Six). There are many different treatment approaches, but a short hospital stay is often required.

Physical Disabilities

These can include a wide range of problems, from juvenile diabetes to cerebral palsy. Adjustments may need to be made in the class schedule or the physical environment so that these children have access to the full education they deserve.

COMMON QUESTIONS PARENTS ASK

Q. The school counselor says our daughter has a learning disorder called dyslexia. He explained that there was something wrong with her brain. What does that mean?

A. Naturally, parents are upset at the thought that their

child could have a learning disability, hyperactivity, or some other disorder that suggests that the brain isn't "working quite right." There are a lot of stigma associated with these conditions, but this isn't fair or accurate. Our brains are like all the other parts of our bodies: every person's brain is a little bit different, and no one's brain is perfect; we just have different strengths and weaknesses. In most cases, we are able to compensate for these differences.

In dyslexia, there are subtle differences in how the brain processes information. For example, it may take your daughter a little longer than the other children in her class to learn reading and writing. But a good remedial program, especially if started early, will help her overcome the problem. It may reassure you (and your child) to know that lots of famous and successful people had problems in school, including Winston Churchill, Albert Einstein, Thomas Edison, Nelson Rockefeller, and Bruce Jenner.

Q. Recently, our son was evaluated by the school psychologist, who said that he has Attention-deficit Hyperactivity Disorder. When she explained the condition and how it should be treated, she talked so fast and used so much jargon we could hardly keep up. We're more confused than ever.

A. Don't be intimidated by the "experts." When a professional uses jargon that you don't understand, ask him or her to define exactly what the word means. If a particular treatment is recommended, be sure you understand it. If you're not satisfied with the therapy, or think the diagnosis is wrong, let the professional know. If necessary, get another opinion. After all, you, too, are an expert about your child.

Speaking of jargon, a small warning: These technical terms help professionals communicate with each other in a kind of shorthand. The problem is that the terms are often misused. When you use a word like dyslexia, or hyperactivity, you may mean one thing, and the teacher or counselor may mean another. It is much better to describe behavior by using specific, concrete terms. For example, if you're worried about your daughter's reading difficulty, describe the problem as precisely as you can. Tell the teacher that she mixes up her letters instead of saying that she is "dyslexic."

CHAPTER 2

COMMUNICATION
IS THE KEY

"Words can brutalize as well as civilize, injure as well as heal. Teachers, like parents, need a language of compassion, a language that lingers lovingly. They need words that convey feelings, responses that change moods, statements that tempt good will, answers that bring insight, replies that radiate respect."

—Dr. Haim Ginott, *Teacher and Child*

IT IS no secret that the vast majority of school problems can be alleviated, even overcome, by improving communication between children, parents, and teachers. It sounds simple, but simple isn't always easy. Good communication means effective listening, and that requires patience and insight as well as a genuine desire to communicate—and not to criticize, cajole, lecture, or blame.

Most parents want to be good communicators, but they don't know how. Others may think they're good communicators. After all, they reason, we're intelligent people, and intelligent people know how to communicate. Unfortunately, they're wrong. The fact is, good communcation is a skill, and like any skill, it must be learned and practiced to be mastered. As parents, we know it is not always easy to open the doors to effective communication and learn what is going on in a child's mind and heart. Years of poor communication habits can't be reversed overnight, and a child who is used to being "tuned out" or lectured at won't suddenly open up when you first try a nonjudgmental, two-way dialogue. But by practicing the following skills, you will be able to improve your communication ability and develop a better parent-child relationship. It may not happen overnight, but be patient and keep trying.

The first step is to examine your listening skills: Are you a good listener? Are you hearing what you child is *not* saying, as well as what he does say? Do you dominate conversation and unintentionally discourage your child from communicating openly? Are the messages you send back helpful or hurtful?

The next step is to get to know your child better. That may sound absurd, but if you're like most parents, you'd be shocked at how little you really know about your child's world.

The third step may surprise you: Get to know yourself. Why do you react the way you do? Are you working too hard at parenting? Are you just repeating patterns you learned from your parents? Or are you blindly reacting against the way you were raised?

The final step is to get know your child's school and teachers. In order to help your child cope with school problems effectively, you will need to have a good objective idea of what the school is like.

If you have any questions or concerns about your child's performance at school, don't hesitate to schedule a meeting with the teacher. Many parents are intimidated by schools and teachers, possibly because of their own negative childhood experiences. Lots of otherwise self-confident adults still get butterflies in the stomach when they walk down a school corridor toward the principal's office. When your child is sent home with a bad report card or punished for some reason, you may be afraid to ask too many questions. Perhaps you're worried that your child will be stigmatized if you meddle in the school's affairs. Maybe you're afraid that people will think you're "babying" your child.

While such fears are common, they're usually groundless. Learning about the school's policies, getting to know the teachers, and being involved in school activities are all positive actions. They should send out a powerful signal to both your child and the school that you are a caring, concerned parent. Of course, if you confront your child's teacher with a hostile, critical attitude, then you probably won't get far. But in most cases, if you approach the teacher with the point of view that you are allies with the common goal of trying to solve your child's problems, you're likely to succeed.

THE FIRST STEP: LEARNING TO LISTEN

Often we think we're communicating with our children because we talk to them a lot. Sometimes when we're watching TV or reading the paper, we go through the motions of talking with our children, dividing our attention between them and some other activity. But remember, the first step in effective communication is to be a good listener.

What is wrong with the following typical exchange between a mother and her 5 year old?

MOTHER: How was kindergarten today?
JENNIFER: Okay.
MOTHER: I bet you had fun, didn't you?
JENNIFER: Yeah . . . I don't know.
MOTHER: You don't know? Wasn't the teacher nice to you?
JENNIFER: Yeah, I guess so.
MOTHER: And didn't you have sing-along today? I bet you liked that, because you really like to sing, don't you?
JENNIFER: Yeah. Singing's fun. Can I play my *Sesame Street* sing-along tape now?

Jennifer and her mother talked, but not much got communicated, because Jennifer's mom steered the conversation with leading questions. There was only one way for Jennifer to answer: She had to agree with her mother, who finished the conversation feeling satisfied that all was well with her little girl. You might have noticed that Jennifer was answering reluctantly. Her mother, however, didn't pick up on her reluctance; instead, she anticipated. Anticipation can short-circuit open communication by limiting, or channeling, our responses.

Let's see how the conversation might have gone if Jennifer's mom had spent more time listening instead of leading:

MOTHER: How was kindergarten today

JENNIFER: Okay.

MOTHER: Just okay?

JENNIFER: Richard knocked over my block house.

MOTHER: How did that make you feel?

JENNIFER: Mad. So I hit him and he started crying.

MOTHER: Oh, I see.

JENNIFER: It was his fault I got mad.

MOTHER: It sounds like maybe you feel bad for hitting him and making him cry.

JENNIFER: Yeah, cause he's my friend. Maybe when he knocked over my blocks it was an accident.

MOTHER: That's possible. Do you think you'd feel better if tomorrow you apologize for hitting him?

JENNIFER: Yeah. If I say I'm sorry, we can still be friends.

In this exchange, Jennifer determined the direction of the conversation. Her mother picked up on the clue that something was on Jennifer's mind, and instead of ignoring that clue, she let her daughter get the problem off her chest. In the first exchange, Jennifer wasn't even given a chance to share her problem. In the second, her mother helped her solve the problem without compounding it by blaming Jennifer for losing her temper. Many parents would have jumped in with a sermon about how naughty it is to hit people. But Jennifer already knew what she had done was wrong. She needed advice on how to solve her problem, not a lecture.

If someone was drowning, you'd throw him a life-preserver, not try to teach him how to swim. But when our children need help, we tend to lecture and criticize. Of course we mean well, but does it help the child? Consider the following exchange between 10-year-old Carl and his father:

CARL: Boy, this English assignment is impossible. We're supposed to make up sentences using all these new words, and I don't even know what half of them mean.

FATHER: Well, if you don't learn how to use a dictionary, you're never going to learn anything. Instead of sitting there complaining, you should be concentrating on your work.

CARL: I *am* concentrating, but it's too hard. I hate English.

What Carl's father said may be partly true, but instead of encouraging, he discouraged. The message he sent to his son was "you're lazy, you're not working hard enough." He also gave his son a lecture that reinforced feelings of frustration and failure, when Carl was hoping for some sympathy. It is easy to see how a conversation like that could quickly escalate into a door-slamming fight.

Let's rewrite the script for that exchange, using more effective communication techniques:

CARL: Boy, this English assignment is impossible. We're supposed to make up sentences using all these new words, and I don't even know what half of them mean.

FATHER: English assignments can be hard work, especially when you have to master a lot of new vocabulary.

CARL: Yeah, it's taking me forever to look up all these words in the dictionary, and I'm afraid I'll forget them before class tomorrow. The teacher said he was going to give us a spelling test.

FATHER: Maybe it would help if you wrote out a list of the new words as you look them up. Then you can review them tomorrow while they're still fresh in your mind.

CARL: That's a good idea—I'll try it.

In the second exchange, the father listened sympathetically. He didn't minimize the difficulty of the task, but still conveyed his confidence that his son could complete it. He responded without blaming or criticizing, and when he offered constructive advice, his son was open to listening to him, too. He gave his son credit for being a responsible and concerned person, and he in turn responded like one.

As this example shows, there are two parts to effective communication: listening sympathetically and responding helpfully. Although most of us are not in the habit, anyone can master effective communication. All it takes is the will and some practice. Throughout this book, we give you examples of good and bad communication styles, and in Chapter Seven, we outline some specific methods for improving your communication skills.

THE SECOND STEP: KNOWING YOUR CHILD

"Last week, Ginny came home from school in tears because her best friend got a róle Ginny had wanted in the Junior Class play. I tried to console her by pointing out that the class play is no big deal anyway, but this just threw Ginny into a rage, shouting that I didn't care about her and that I didn't understand anything anyway. Of course I feel bad that she didn't get the part if she really wanted it so badly—but I didn't know that she was the least bit interested. She never even told us that she had joined the Drama Club."

This story illustrates a surprising fact about most of us: We really don't know very much about our children's lives outside the home. When our children are very young, of course, the home and family are virtually the whole universe to the child. But when children start school, other people, especially friends and teachers, start to play increasingly important roles. The older the child gets, the more important outside influences become, for better or for worse. Unless you work to keep the channels of communication open, there will be whole segments of your child's life that you don't know anything about.

That is what happened with Ginny and her parents: she never had any big problems at school, so they tended to leave well enough alone. They rarely asked her about her extracurricular activities. She was popular, had nice friends, and got decent grades, so why worry?

But from Ginny's viewpoint, there was a problem: Her parents were tuning her out. It's no wonder that Ginny was hurt when her mother said, "Oh well, the Junior Class play is no big deal." For Ginny, it *was* a big deal—she had worked hard for the tryouts and she really wanted the part. If her mother had known how important it was to her, she would have been more sensitive and better able to help Ginny accept her disappointment.

Like most parents, Ginny's mother needs to spend some time discovering what it is that her child does during those six to eight hours she is away from home every day. We're not advocating that you supervise every moment of your child's life. That would be both unrealistic and inappropriate. It is unrealistic because you can't be with your child all day long, while he is at school or with friends or at Scout meetings. It is inappropriate because growing up to be a healthy, mature adult requires learning to be independent from your parents. But you shouldn't go to the other extreme either, throwing up your hands and saying, "Well, he's in school now, and there's not much I can do about what happens when I'm not there. I will just hope for the best and pray that he gets a good teacher and makes nice friends."

The best place to start learning about your child's "other" life is with your child. Try asking him how his day went and what he did at school. Did he have any funny conversations with his friends, or did anything unusual happen? Reading this, you're probably reacting like Claudia's mother: "If only it was that easy. I ask my daughter how school was and she says, 'Okay, I guess.' Then she throws her backpack on the couch, turns on the TV, and gets on the phone with a girlfriend for a forty-five-minute marathon conversation about whatever it was that didn't happen that day."

Really getting to know your child—what delights him, what frightens him, what motivates him—is a long-term, ongoing process. It requires patience, dedication, and the effective communication skills that we refer to throughout this book. The following self-test, "How Well Do You Know Your Child?" is not a substitute for communication skills, but it can help you get started. To do this exercise, take a piece of paper and jot down how you think your child would complete each of the statements. You and your spouse may want to complete the test separately, to see if you come up with the same responses. When you're finished, go over the questions with your child and see what he or she answers. Of course, the answers will change as your child grows up, so you may want to repeat the test from time to time.

Don't bother trying to score this test—there are no right or wrong answers. The point is simply to let you assess how well you know your child's world, and how well you understand how he or she relates to it. The discussion you have with your child afterward can provide you with valuable insights. One warning, however: Don't start lecturing your child about his responses, and don't try to impose your tastes and desires on him. You may wish that your son preferred Mozart to Motley Crue, or you may be shocked that your 11-year-old daughter's favorite female star is Madonna, but trying to impose your will is counterproductive.

SELF-TEST: HOW WELL DO YOU KNOW YOUR CHILD?

My grades are

My best friend is

My worst enemy is

My favorite teacher is

My least favorite teacher is

My favorite subject is

My least favorite subject is

My favorite piece of clothing is

My favorite book is

My favorite movie is

My favorite food is

My favorite music is

My favorite sport is

My favorite stars/role models are

   (1) male

   (2) female

My goals are

   (1) for this year

   (2) for my career

My favorite activities are

My idea of a perfect vacation is

The purpose of the exercise is not to pass judgment: instead, it's an opportunity to learn more about your child. If you use the exercise as an excuse to lecture or criticize, it will backfire. Take, for example, the story told by 17-year-old Justin.

There's that one question about long-term goals, you know, what do you want to be when you grow up. Dumbly, I told the truth: that I'm not sure yet. What a mistake. My mother starts moaning about how I better make up my mind soon, 'cause I'm gonna have to choose a college and decide on a major, and my father starts yelling about how when he was my age, he was working four hours a day after school and all day Saturday to save money so he could go to pharmacy school. They didn't care about how I felt, they just wanted an excuse to tell me what to do, which is to be a pharmacist, just like Dad."

Justin felt, and rightly so, that his parents had manipulated him. He opened a door to communication, but they slammed it shut with their lecturing. This made Justin resentful, but even worse, his parents missed an important opportunity to get to know him better. When Justin admitted that he didn't know what career he wanted to pursue, they could have explored the question calmly, without focusing on the negative aspects of Justin's indecisiveness.

THE THIRD STEP: KNOW YOURSELF

We don't mean "know yourself" in a superficial, simplistic way, where you define yourself in terms of what you do or where you live or how much money you make. Rather, know yourself in terms of your values, your beliefs, and your traditions What is truly important to you? What values do you most want to pass on to your children? What sorts of personal achievements really matter to you?

None of these questions can be answered easily. In fact, most of us tend not to think about them too often, or when we do, we're not sure how to find the answers. You may wonder: What does this have to do with communicating with my child? Although many factors influence a child's development, parents are the single most important role model. Whether we are conscious of it or not, we are constantly projecting our own self-images and world views to our children. By thinking clearly about who you are and what you care about, you will be able to provide a much more positive and coherent message for your child.

We are not saying that you should put on an act, pretending to be someone different or better than you believe yourself to be. Just the opposite, in fact. You should be providing your child with a parental role model that says, This is who we are, this is what we value, these are our moral standards. We're proud of who we are, even if we're not always perfect. We do the best we can, and when we make mistakes, we try to correct them. Your standards may be different from the family down the street, but the important thing is that you project your values consistently, so that your child can develop a positive, healthy self-image.

Most of us are not in the habit of introspection. In fact, many people think that it is egotistical and self-indulgent to spend too much time thinking about yourself. As psychiatrists, we've both heard plenty of parents say, "There's nothing wrong with us—it's our son [or daughter] who's got the problem. What difference does it make how I feel about my schooling when he's the one who got suspended?" The answer is that much of our children's behavior is determined by the signals we send out— consciously or unconsciously. We can't really understand that behavior—or that child—until we understand ourselves.

Knowing who you are and what you want for your child opens the door to communication, although it doesn't guarantee that your child will act just the way you hope. What it will do is give you a more rational framework for communicating with each other. In addition to helping you see what things you really care about, thinking about your own upbringing can help you identify negative attitudes that may be hindering your relationship with your child. You may be carrying around tired old attitudes and responses you learned from your parents and that you now unconsciously apply to your own children.

Learning about ourselves, like learning about our children, is an ongoing process that is never really complete. One helpful way to start the process is to spend a quiet hour or two reviewing and assessing your own upbringing. Like the self-test "How Well Do You Know Your Child," this exercise can help you reach some surprising insights about your own childhood and adult attitudes—and these insights can help you understand your own child better, as well.

A good way to help you begin your assessment is to divide a piece of paper into 4 parts:

WHO   WHAT   ACTUAL   IDEAL

In the lefthand column, jot down names of people (parents, relatives, teachers) and institutions (school, church, sports teams, Scouts, etc.) that were important in your childhood. Concentrate on listing people who had an impact on your upbringing. This might include figures from the immediate family, as well as grandparents and uncles and aunts. Don't worry about trying to remember everyone or everything; you can always add more names later. The order of the names doesn't matter either.

Next, in the "WHAT" column, write down one or two words that characterize how you think that person (or institution) affected your upbringing and shaped how you feel about yourself. Again, this doesn't have to be comprehensive; as you go through your list, you may want to come back to an earlier note and refine it.

Now, looking over your list, make a note in the "ACTUAL" column about whether you think a particular person has affected your own parenting style and attitudes. If the effect is positive, put a plus; if it's negative, put a minus. Would you like any of these influences to have been different? Do you wish, for example, that you had inherited more of your grandfather's sense of fair play, and less of Aunt Lucy's short temper? Note these observations with pluses and minuses in the "ideal" column.

Again, there are no right or wrong answers. This is just a tool to help you review your own past experiences and see how they may affect the way you behave and respond as a parent. Once you understand these influences, you will be better able to control and modify them.

The way we ourselves were raised tends to affect our own parenting styles in one of two diametrically opposed ways, although most of us combine some of both patterns. One pattern is to do certain things because that's what our parents did, and we can't imagine things being done differently. The second pattern is to reject certain things our parents did, swearing to ourselves that we will never subject our children to thus and such. In this second pattern, we tend to become strict where our parents were lenient, or lenient where they were strict.

Paradoxically, many of us combine both patterns of rejecting and accepting our parents' child-rearing styles. When it comes to reading, for example, you may say, "I learned to read at age four, and by golly, my child's going to be reading in kindergarten, too." But when it comes to clothes, you take a lenient tack: "My mother made me wear such nerdy clothes, I always felt out of it. I'm going to let my kids wear whatever they want." When it comes to music lessons, your disciplinarian streak may rule: "My mother never made me practice the piano, so I never progressed. I'm going to give my children the support and structure I wish I'd had."

None of these approaches is necessarily right or wrong. The question is, which one is right for you and your child? Sometimes it's right to be permissive; sometimes it's right to be strict. What's right for one parent may not be right for the other, and what's right for one child may not be right for another. The only way to know is by examining your actions and motivations objectively, and thinking through how the child is likely to respond.

THE FOURTH STEP: KNOW YOUR SCHOOL

School is another important influence in your child's life. After all, from the earliest grades on, children spend close to a third of their time in class, doing homework, or involved with other school-related activities. In fact, your children probably spend a lot more of their waking hours involved with school than they spend with you. You have a right, and even an obligation, to be familiar with your child's school and teachers. This is especially important when your child is having problems, because you can't solve those problems until you have an objective understanding of their context.

If your daughter failed a class, why did this happen? Did she not study hard enough? Was she a discipline problem? Does she have a learning disability? Maybe the teacher or the school is at fault. The only way you can know is by knowing the school.

Talk to the teachers and the administrators. Learn about the school's policies and educational philosophy. If necessary, ask if you can observe for a day. Your child may object at first—especially if you've never shown much interest in the school before. You have to demonstrate that your involvement with the school is evidence of your love and commitment—not a sign that you don't trust him and are checking up on him.

When your child has problems at school, it is possible that the school's policy and educational outlook may be contributing to the difficulty. Many schools today use the "management systems" approach to teaching, and this can easily increase the sense of stress and anxiety a child feels at school. As you might guess from the name, management systems is a concept borrowed from business. It has been introduced in response to the public perception that schools are failing to teach our children the basics, and that schools should be more accountable for the performance of their students. Because grades and test scores are the most objective way of measuring achievement, management systems focus on testing in basic competency areas, such as reading, vocabulary, composition, and arithmetic. The teacher and the school's performance are assessed on the basis of their students' test scores. If the students do well, then the teachers and the school are judged to have succeeded.

It is easy to imagine how such a system could make teachers feel anxious, and they're bound to pass this anxiety on to their students. After all, the student's score reflects not just on himself, but also on his teacher. Another drawback of this approach is that it tends to emphasize the acquisition of skills rather than their application. Therefore, the child is under a great deal of pressure to achieve, but he isn't necessarily inspired to learn.

If your school uses this system, you may need to remind your child (and maybe yourself!) that grades are not the sole purpose of school. Learning is. Grades are just a method schools use to quantify and compare a child's achievements against the expected standards. Teachers and schools use grades to track each student's progress as objectively as possible, but even they know the system is imperfect. (But teachers will point out that parents rarely complain that a high grade was unearned!) If you think a grade is unfair, talk to the teacher about what went into his or her decision to give it. We're not suggesting that you shouldn't be concerned if your child's report card is filled with D's; a child who is failing, or close to it, is certainly in need of help. But do you expect your child to make only A's and B's? In most schools, "C" means fair or average, and it is reasonable to assume that it is therefore the most common grade on report cards all over the country.

What should you do if you think the school is at fault in your child's problems? To begin with, avoid blaming and finger-pointing. This is no more productive with a teacher than it is when communicating with your child. Keep an open mind, and try to get the facts. Look at how 8-year-old Tony's parents responded when his teacher sent a note home saying that Tony was boisterous and disruptive in class, and must learn to control his behavior. Tony's father's immediate response was irritation: "That teacher's a dried up old prune. Tony's a great kid—he's just having fun, and he's doing okay in his schoolwork. I was pretty wild as a kid, too, and I turned out all right." Wisely, Tony's parents didn't call and confront the teacher while they were heated up, nor did they put her down in front of Tony. The next day, they scheduled a conference with the teacher, and when they met, they calmly explained their concern: what she saw as disruptive behavior, they felt was just normal 8-year-old playfulness.

Parents and teachers can have very different perspectives on a child's behavior. That doesn't necessarily mean that the teacher is right and the parents are wrong—or vice versa. But frequently, the stresses and structure of the classroom can highlight or intensify a child's weaknesses. A quiet, shy child may become completely withdrawn when he starts a new school; an outgoing, high-spirited child may become restless and fidgety when he has to sit behind a desk working alone for long stretches of time. You may not be bothered by the fact that your child hums and whistles and jiggles his leg while he solves arithmetic problems, but the teacher has to consider the needs of the other students in the class, and that kind of behavior can be very distracting.

Unfortunately, not all schools and teachers are ideal. There are rigid, oppressive school systems that reward only conformity and obedience; there are thoughtless teachers who belittle children and squelch their creative urges. Luckily, these are the exceptions, and you shouldn't complain about the teacher or the school unless you've made a genuine attempt to get help for your child. Most teachers and schools are dedicated and well-meaning, if occasionally less than perfect. When troubles come up, approach the school with the understanding that you are partners in your child's education and social growth. You should expect the best teaching and support possible for your child, but you should also respect the teacher's own pressures and restraints.

Make sure that you're not expecting too much from the school. Many families today are under a lot of social and economic strain, and they expect the school to act as a surrogate parent. The idealized families of postwar television shows, such as *Father Knows Best* and *Leave It To Beaver* with their full-time, stay-at-home moms, have pretty much vanished. More common nowadays are families in which both parents work—sometimes because the mother feels social pressure to pursue a career, but more often because of economic need. Increases in the divorce rate have also had a major impact, leaving single parents to struggle alone with all the stresses of work and parenting.

These pressures have forced many parents to give up responsibility and authority over the day-to-day activities of their children. In his book *The Hurried Child*, the respected child psychologist David Elkind argues that our modern world, with its economic pressures and social stresses, encourages us to ignore our children's needs. In fact, the phenomenon of children coming home from school to an empty house has become so common that there's a term for it: these are latchkey kids. Parents are justifiably worried about leaving their kids unsupervised for hours every day. Without parental guidance, children are vulnerable to a host of problems, and it is not realistic to expect the schools to fill this gap.

MAKING TIME FOR TALK

Getting to know more about your child, yourself, and the school will take time, but it is not impossible. You're probably saying, but I don't have any extra time! You have to make time to start communicating effectively with your child. We say make time, not find it, because your children must be your number-one priority. We both know from personal experience how hard that is, especially in two-working-parent households. Between job demands and the chores that need to be done at home, precious little time is left over to spend just talking with our families. Maybe you could arrange for flexible or staggered working hours that would give you more time at home when the children are out of school, or perhaps you could hire someone to do yard work or clean the house so that your weekends aren't tied up with chores. If you can't afford those luxuries, try to turn necessary chores into family activities. Instead of rushing through the shopping mall, take time out to browse together in a bookstore or pick out a video to watch together that evening. If you have more than one child, try to spend a little time each week with each child alone. Most important, when you do have time to spend with your children, don't waste it on fruitless bickering and nagging. Invest your valuable time in getting to know each other better.

CHAPTER 3

THE EARLY YEARS: LEARNING TO LET GO

OBVIOUSLY, THE early years—ages two to six—are very important years in your child's life. During these years, your child faces many exciting challenges involving the initial separation from parents. Although it may be difficult for a parent with a screaming toddler to view the leaving of the child with a [pick one] babysitter, day care attendant, nursery school teacher, mother-in-law, as an "exciting challenge," the vast majority of parents and children quickly overcome their initial separation anxiety.

For a *few* families, however, separation proves especially difficult. In this chapter, we describe four children who had trouble separating themselves from their parents when they first started school. The cases may seem different on the surface, but on a deeper level, they're very similar. You may even recognize your own child's behavior in one of them.

We also discuss two other children, whose cases illustrate important problems that can occur in the early years. One involves Attention-deficit Hyperactivity Disorder (ADHD), which affects a relatively large number of schoolchildren. The other case raises a question most parents worry about: "When should my child start reading?"

The way a child responds to kindergarten and first grade can affect his whole school experience. The reading and arithmetic skills he learns will be the building blocks for the rest of his schoolwork. Parents can help, not by senseless pushing, but by creating an atmosphere that encourages good study habits. Later in the book, we talk about some specific things you can do to encourage good homework skills. But even if your child isn't getting regular homework assignments yet, you can spend time together building patience, perseverance, and a love of learning. These qualities will make school a pleasure in later years.

The development of social skills, both at school and at home, cannot be ignored either. Making and keeping friends, sharing, playing by the rules, and learning to be part of a team are just as important to children as to adults. It is these social skills that will determine how your child interacts with other children. What your child learns as a youngster sets the stage for getting along with other people as an adult.

Now, let's look at some case histories, to see what causes problems and how they can be solved.

JAMES: WHOSE PROBLEM IS THIS, ANYHOW?

James puts up a huge fuss every morning when his mother drops him off at kindergarten. Although she tries to reassure him that he will be okay, James cries and whimpers, clinging to her legs. Because of these scenes, his mother has been late to work four times this week.

At first, James's story sounds like nothing more than the typical separation anxiety that occurs at this stage. It is natural, and even healthy, for a 5-year-old to be upset when he is left at kindergarten—in his view, abandoned by his parents.

But there is something worrisome about this case: James's mother says the problem has been getting worse, not better. In most cases, the child will get *better* adjusted to the separation over time. There is no evidence that something's wrong with the school or teacher. So let's analyze the way his mother is dealing with the situation.

"I knew James would have trouble adjusting to kindergarten," she said. "He's always been very attached to me. In fact, I didn't even want to go back to work, but my husband insisted. I agreed to give it a try, but if I'm going to be late all the time, I will be out of a job anyway."

A Mixed Message

James's mother does not seem certain that she wants to work. In fact, it almost sounds as if she wants to use James's problem as an excuse to quit—or even get fired! She talks about how much her son needs her. Of course he does need her—but does he need her as much as she thinks? James is growing up, and growing up means becoming independent. James's mother is afraid to let go—and as long as she won't let go, James will be afraid to separate himself from her, too. *Although they shouldn't be hurried into growing up, children need support and encouragement to become independent.*

THE MANY EXPRESSIONS OF SEPARATION ANXIETY

Separation anxiety is most common when the child first starts school, but it can be seen in other situations, too. These problems may seem very different from one another, but they can all be expressions of a child's instinctive fear of being separated from his parents.

Staying with a babysitter

Joining a playgroup

Playing in a room alone (even if mother is in the house)

Sleeping away from home

Worrying about being lost, kidnapped, or hurt

Asking for Trouble

James's mother said she "knew James would have trouble adjusting," but this may have become a self-fulfilling prophecy. Because she believed it, she sent out subtle signals to James that said, I expect you to be afraid at school.

We asked her exactly what she tells James to help him adjust to school. "I've tried everything. At first, I just said he shouldn't be scared, that everything would be okay. I also explained that I didn't want to leave him but that I had to go away. Nothing worked. Now it's gotten to the point that I have to promise to stay for a while—then, when he's distracted, I leave. But last time he started up again as soon as I went to say good-bye."

Far from encouraging him to separate from her and adjust to kindergarten, James's mother is reinforcing his anxiety. In fact, the way she's reacting to his fussing and clinging at kindergarten is part of the problem. The only thing she has accomplished is to increase James's fears about being away from her.

A Two-Part Solution

This problem has to be approached on two levels.

Self-knowledge. First, James's mother has to come to terms with her feelings about going to work, instead of projecting her discomfort onto James. She and her husband need to communicate openly and honestly about her job. Is she working because they need the second income? Or is it because of social pressure for her to have a "career" instead of being "just a housewife?"

She may decide to stay home—or to continue working. But whichever she does, she must make peace with her decision. And whatever her decision, James still has to go to kindergarten. He can't stay dependent on his mother forever, and she should ease the separation as well as she can.

Letting go. The second part of the solution is that James's mother has to rearrange how she leaves him at kindergarten. Her current style encourages James's dependency instead of helping him learn to be independent. For example, she hangs around until James settles down and gets involved with the other children's activities.

It may be okay to stay in the room for a while during the first few days of kindergarten. At that point, your child really isn't sure what to expect, and he may need the reassurance of knowing that you are there. James should be past that point, but his mother has been too sheltering and overprotective. As a result, he hasn't learned that he can be without her for a pretty long stretch of time. One thing he has learned, however, is that he can manipulate his mother into staying longer if he cries and clings to her.

Overcoming Your Own Anxiety

We advised James's mother to be firm about leaving as soon as she delivers James to the teacher. "But he will get so upset and cry even more!" she objected. That's probably true—at first. But he will eventually come to terms with it. *The important thing is that his mother must be consistent.* If James learns that she will give in and stay when he makes enough of a fuss, he will never adjust.

Children are not the only ones to suffer separation anxiety—parents do, too. It's hard to let go as our children grow up. But the greatest gift we can give them is the self-confidence they need to become emotionally mature adults. If your child is having trouble adjusting to nursery or kindergarten, are you aggravating the problem with your own fears?

SEPARATION ANXIETY: A TWO-WAY STREET

As we discussed, many parents have trouble letting go and accepting their children's growing independence. One of our favorite stories is told by a friend of ours, who felt guilty when she left her 4-year-old at home with a sitter so that she could resume her career as a nurse.

"Every morning, there would be a big scene: Gretchen would be sobbing and I'd be trying to soothe her, but she'd just keep on crying. I could hear her weeping from outside as I locked the door, and I'd leave for work feeling so guilty, like a rotten mother. But, at the end of day, the sitter would always say that Gretchen was fine after I left."

"One day, I decided to do a test. I went through all the motions of going to work—putting on my coat, doing the long farewell and everything. But instead of leaving, I just slammed the front door and stayed inside. Gretchen had been in the kitchen with the sitter, crying her eyes out. Suddenly it was silent. Then, after a few seconds, I heard Gretchen's voice saying, 'Okay, Mommy's gone. We can play now.'

Of course, Gretchen was genuinely upset that her mother was leaving. But she had learned to accept it and trusted that her mother would come back. Her mother, however, had not overcome her *own* separation anxiety. As a result, the ritual good-bye in the mornings had become more painful and prolonged than necessary. Gretchen was just reacting as her mother expected (and probably hoped!) she would.

JOSHUA: BAD NIGHTS, BAD MORNINGS

Six-year-old Joshua dawdles endlessly every morning before school. His parents cannot get him to speed up, although he has plenty of energy in the afternoons and evenings. Joshua's father describes breakfast as "slow torture." "He practically eats his cereal one flake at a time. Then, when he's supposed to be brushing his teeth, I will find him lying down in the hall, petting the dog. Or I tell him to go get his jacket, and when he gets to the closet, he decides he has to change his shirt. It's nearly impossible to get him to leave for school on time."

Joshua's mother adds, "He's so slow and daydreamy in the mornings. I can't tell if he's doing it deliberately or not. I wonder if it's because he's not sleeping well; he has been waking up a lot lately in the middle of the night, because of nightmares. But he seems to have plenty of pep in the afternoons, when he comes home."

The first order of business in this case was to obtain a complete pediatric examination. This is critical any time a child has symptoms, such as tiredness or fatigue, that could be caused by a physical condition. In Joshua's case, there was no physical cause, so we next looked for psychological reasons for his behavior. His parents suspected that his dawdling was somehow connected to his nightmares. After some digging and talking, we discovered that was partly true. "He started this morning foot-dragging routine at the same time as the nightmares began," his father related. "That was just before school started."

Too Many Assumptions

Joshua's mother chimed in, "He just started at public school—before he went to nursery and kindergarten at our church. But it's a couple of miles away, so we had to drive him back and forth. The public school is much better—it's only a block away from here, so he can walk."

His father added, "We thought Josh would love the new school, but he doesn't seem that excited about it. It's a great big modern building, and they've got excellent facilities, including lots of computers for the kids to use."

Underestimating Stress

Joshua's problem is practically the opposite of James's. James was overprotected. But Joshua's parents are underestimating the stress their son is under. They're looking at his situation from their own points of view. Joshua's mother is pleased that he can walk to the school, and his father is impressed by the school's amenities.

We suggested that Joshua's parents look at the problem through his own eyes. Schools can be intimidating places. This large institution is probably pretty scary to little Joshua, especially after coming from the small, sheltered nursery and kindergarten at the church.

Getting to Joshua's Fears

Using the effective communication techniques presented in Chapter Two, Joshua's parents talked to him about his feelings about school. They didn't make assumptions about how much he must like it (because they do); they simply listened to him. One thing they found out was that Joshua didn't like walking to school alone because he was afraid he would be kidnapped.

Joshua's parents were shocked. Their first instinct was to tell him that his fear was silly. But instead of turning him off by glossing over his fears, they kept the lines of communication open.

They learned that at the end of the summer, he had seen a television program about a little boy who was kidnapped from the playground at school. He had associated this with starting at the new school. As we mentioned earlier, separation anxiety can sometimes be expressed as a fear of being kidnapped or getting lost. Also, Joshua was intimidated by this big new school with all its classrooms and corridors and hundreds of older children.

Underlying Anxieties

Why didn't Joshua tell his parents about his fears sooner? It may be because they were so sure that there were no problems, that they didn't provide an opening for him. So instead of confronting it directly, Joshua tried to ignore his anxiety—and it came out in the form of nightmares. Also, children (and adults, too!) don't always know exactly what it is that's troubling them. You need to make time to talk, because sometimes it takes a while for these connections to surface.

Confronting His Fears

Joshua's parents dealt with the problem very well: they simply encouraged him to talk openly about his anxieties, especially about being kidnapped. They discussed what he should do if a stranger ever did come up to him, and how they would call the police if he was late coming from school one day. Joshua seemed relieved just to be able to talk about his fears.

Once the channels of communication were open, Joshua's parents were more tuned in to their son's anxieties. By dealing with them openly, Joshua was able to overcome them. Soon the nightmares became less and less common. And now that he had confronted his fears, there was no reason for Joshua to dawdle in the mornings; he looked forward to getting to school, instead of trying to put it off.

KIMBERLY: THE STRESS OF DIVORCE

Kimberly is a popular, bright 7-year-old girl who adjusted beautifully to kindergarten and loved school in first grade. But suddenly, at the start of second grade, she refuses to leave the house to go to school. Her mother can't understand why this is happening. "Kimberly has always been eager to please," her mother told us. "Maybe that's why she adjusted to school so well. But now we have a big battle every morning: she has a headache, or her stomach hurts, or she has some other excuse. I'd almost think it was fear of being separated from me, but she's too old for that. Besides, she didn't have any problems in kindergarten or first grade. She's been clinging to me like a two-year-old ever since my husband and I were separated in July."

Just because Kimberly didn't experience separation anxiety when she started school doesn't mean that it can't be happening now. Separation anxiety is most common when a child first goes to school, but it can appear at any age. It's especially likely to surface if there's some other stressful event in the child's life. In

Kimberly's case, it's not at all surprising that separation anxiety would appear now, just after her father moved out.

Divorce and separation are traumatic events for any child; it is truly a tragedy that so many children in our society are subjected to it. Children thrive on stability. When parents break up, the child feels very threatened. Unfortunately, divorce cannot always be prevented. But when it happens, you should take special care to recognize your child's insecurities and help the child through this troubling time.

Displaced Fear

"But why would Kimberly be afraid to go school," Kimberly's mother asked, "if what she's upset about is that her father has moved out?" The answer is that children often don't know how to express their feelings and their fears. Like adults, they may feel something unconsciously, but not be able to express it. Besides, refusing to *go to* school doesn't necessarily mean that something is wrong *at* school. It's more likely that Kimberly is afraid that if she is separated from her mother, she may lose her, too—the same way she lost her father.

Misplaced Guilt

It's very important to understand how a child Kimberly's age views the world, and what she thinks is cause and effect. She is still young enough to believe that somehow she was to blame for her father leaving. Young children are egotistical. That doesn't mean they are conceited, but that they normally tend to see themselves as *being at the center of the universe*. They can't easily see things from other people's points of view.

Kimberly was, in her mother's words, "eager to please." But even though she tried to be good, her father still moved out. According to Kimberly's child-based logic, this was a rejection of her. Now she's afraid that her mother might reject her, too.

Coping with Divorce

It will take time and patience to resolve this problem. Kimberly's mother—*and* father—have to reassure her that she was not to blame for the separation. She also has to be reassured that her father hasn't rejected her. Her parents should let her know that no matter what, they both love her. She particularly needs to be sure that her mother is not going to leave her, too. When Kimberly feels more secure about her relationship with her parents, she will be less afraid of being physically away from her mother at school.

Schools and Divorce

Kimberly's mother should also talk to the teacher about the fact that she and Kimberly's father have separated. The teacher doesn't need to know any private details, but it is important for him or her to understand that Kimberly is under this kind of stress. With patient reassurance from both parents, Kimberly will get over her anxiety about leaving for school. In the meantime, her mother should gently but firmly insist that she go to school every day. Letting her stay home with made-up headaches and stomachaches only perpetuates the problem.

ROBBIE: THE CHILD TORNADO

Robbie is a real ball of fire. His father says he's all boy, but his first-grade teacher says he's part boy and part tornado. Robbie can be cute, but his teacher has gotten fed up with his nonstop energy. He's constantly in and out of his seat, and his restlessness distracts the other children.

When Robbie first came to our office with his parents, there was no way of missing him. He was tearing around the waiting room as if it were an obstacle course, until his parents finally got him to sit down. Next, he leafed through every magazine on the coffee table. Soon, he was up again—this time at the receptionist's desk, where he wanted to know about everything.

"What's that?" he asked, pointing to the blinking lights on the phone console. Then he asked, "Can I play with the computer?" He reached for it before he heard the answer, which was no! If this was what he was like in school, no wonder his teacher was exasperated—and the other children distracted.

Hyperactivity

This kind of nonstop activity, with almost uncontrollable bursts of energy, is a common symptom of Attention-deficit Hyperactivity Disorder, which we discussed in Chapter One. It's also common that the disorder is first noticed in first grade. Actually, there may have been signs earlier than first grade, but the problem often isn't noticed until the child is in a structured environment, like school. Before, the child could run around and burn off a lot of the energy; no one really expected him to sit still and concentrate.

Boys Will Be Boys

Robbie's parents said he had always been very active—even aggressive. "He's always been much wilder and noisier than our older two, but they're girls." Robbie's father added, "You expect a boy to be like that—you know, a little macho man. His sisters are very quiet and feminine."

We noted earlier that most of the problems we talk about in this book are just as likely to occur in either boys or girls. But Attention-deficit Hyperactivity Disorder, ADHD, is an exception. For some reason, this problem is much more common in boys. Because we all too often believe that "boys will be boys," diagnosis of this disorder can be missed until the child is older. Parents, and even teachers, sometimes brush off symptoms of hyperactivity because they think it's just high spirits or immaturity or a phase that will pass.

Safe, Effective Treatment

It is lucky that Robbie's problem was noticed so early. This way, he can get started on treatment before he starts to fall behind the other children in his class. He may also need some extra help at school. ADHD is not a "true" learning disorder (like, for example, dyslexia), but it can make it hard for the child to focus on schoolwork.

Robbie will need extra attention and understanding from his parents—and they will need to learn about coping with this disorder. Besides difficulties with school, children with ADHD also tend to have trouble emotionally and socially. They can be too aggressive, and may have trouble making and keeping friends. But again, because the problem was noticed so early, the outlook for Robbie is excellent.

IS YOUR CHILD HYPERACTIVE?

A high energy level is not the only symptom of Attention-deficit Hyperactivity Disorder. You should suspect a problem if your child has any combination (usually six or more) of the following symptoms for a long period of time.

- Distractibility
- Impulsiveness
- Restlessness
- Disorganization
- Poor memory
- Short attention span
- Short temper
- Uncontrollable energy
- Physical recklessness
- Aggressiveness
- Lack of self-control
- Difficulty following rules
- Stubbornness
- Disobedience

CAITLIN: WHY CAN'T SHE READ?

Caitlin, who just started first grade, doesn't show much interest in reading. In fact, she's not very good at it. The teacher isn't worried. In a note to her parents, he wrote, "Caitlin does have some reading skills, so there's no reason to think she has either a physical problem or a learning disorder that interferes with her ability to read. She's just not quite 'ready' psychologically."

Still, her parents *are* worried: their three older children were all reading above grade level when they were Caitlin's age. They're starting to wonder if she has a learning disability.

Caitlin's parents' concern is understandable—and appropriate. Reading is the single most important academic skill your child will develop. It's better to be safe than sorry any time you suspect a learning disability: if Caitlin falls behind her classmates, she will have trouble catching up.

MYTHS AND MISINFORMATION ABOUT HYPERACTIVITY

A lot has been written about Attention-deficit Hyperactivity Disorder, but unfortunately, a lot of it has been false and misleading. It may even have stopped you from getting your child help.

Don't believe all the scare stories you hear about stimulant medications such as Ritalin, Dexedrine, and Cylert that are often used to treat the disorder. They are generally quite safe when given under a doctor's regular supervision and they do not:

- Cause addiction
- "Knock out" or sedate the child
- Cover up or suppress "unacceptable" behavior
- Replace the need for remedial work and behavioral therapy
- Suppress long-term growth

Special diets have been advocated by some specialists, but scientific studies have shown that they are ineffective.

What's the Right Age to Start Reading?

You should expect your child to be reading, at least minimally, by the end of first grade. Otherwise, something is wrong. It could be a physical problem, such as poor eyesight or eye-muscle coordination; a perceptual difficulty, such as dyslexia; or an emotional problem, such as poor self-esteem.

Even though Caitlin's teacher wasn't too concerned, her parents went ahead and asked for an evaluation by the school counselor. As it turned out, Caitlin's reading skills are about average for her grade. The real problem is that Caitlin's parents are expecting her to be *ahead* of her grade level, since their older children were. Caitlin has just started first grade, so she's not behind schedule; she simply isn't very interested in reading yet. In this case, the teacher is right. It will be best to take a wait-and-see approach, at least for a couple of months.

Pushing Too Hard

It is possible that Caitlin is not "ready"—or interested—because her parents are pushing her too hard. Instead of asking, "When will Caitlin read?" her parents should be asking, "How can we help Caitlin learn to love reading?" Her parents are pressuring her to read—like her older brothers and sister. To Caitlin, reading seems like a task, not a pleasure. She doesn't understand why she needs to read, except that it's something her parents want.

Like most parents, Caitlin's mother and father know how important it is to build reading skills by reading aloud to their children. But they were taking "helping" and "encouraging" too far with Caitlin. She didn't take to reading as quickly as their older children. But instead of relaxing and letting Caitlin set the pace, they started to push harder, even using flash cards and other reading aids.

Make Reading Fun

Our advice in this case was to let up the pressure. *It's generally best to leave the structured teaching to the school and encourage reading by making it pleasant and comfortable.* For example, give each child a special place for his own books—even if it's just a spot on a shelf. Schedule a daily family time for reading—for example, while you read the paper after dinner. Or try to mesh reading with your child into your daily activites, such as:

Reading the TV listings (or movie reviews) together to decide what's worth watching.

Reading the captions of newspaper cartoons

Looking through the newspaper ads for a toy or item of clothing your child wants.

Read the sports pages to see how your local team did

Reading the instructions on a new board game.

Looking for familiar words on cereal boxes, soup cans, etc. Whatever you do, remember to make it fun—not drudgery.

QUESTIONS PARENTS ASK

Q. My kids are both fairly good readers, but they're terrible at arithmetic. How can we help improve their number skills?

A. There are dozens of exercises that can be done to help children build up their number skills. As with reading, an understanding of numbers is a basic skill. Arithmetic is essential to the businessman or scientist, but everyone uses it for day-to-day activities: figuring out the household budget, doing taxes, picking the best interest rate, determining how long it will take to drive somewhere. Try to make arithmetic fun by incorporating it into your daily activities: play math games with the silverware, pieces of fruit, measuring cups, etc. Let your children share in the process, so they can see how important numbers are in everyday life.

Q. Our daughter is three and half. When should we teach her to read?

A. There's no simple answer to this question. Ideally, reading should be taught when your child is ready. Some children want to read when they're quite young, but others don't want to read until they're older. There is no reason to be concerned if your child isn't in the early reading group; early readers aren't necessarily any brighter than later ones. Just because a child starts reading earlier does not mean that he or she will always be a better reader than a child who started later.

Q. Doesn't early reading give kids a "head start" so that they do better in school all along?

A. Children who learn to read early do seem to have an edge over their classmates in the early grades. But most studies show that reading skills tend to even out pretty quickly as children get past the first few grades. In fact, one well-known study (conducted by Carleton Washburn in the 1930s at the Winnetka, Illinois public schools) indicates that it may not help to push reading too early. That study suggested that children who started reading when they were older tended to enjoy reading more than children who learned to read when they were very young.

SUMMARY OF THE EARLY YEARS

The one guiding principle you should apply at this stage is to give your child plenty of support, attention, and love. Recognize his achievements and interests. At the same time, you must let him start to assert his independence. Be sensitive to the developmental stages your child is going through, so that you can recognize whether problems are developing. And if there is a problem, don't blame—*communicate.*

CHAPTER 4

THE MIDDLE YEARS: LEARNING TO BELONG

SCHOOL BECOMES even more important between the ages of seven and eleven. These are the years when the child builds on skills learned in kindergarten and first grade. If he has fallen behind you can help him catch up now.

This is also a critical time socially, and peer pressure can be very powerful. You should make sure that your child develops healthy friendships. This means friends who will support him, not exploit him, and who will contribute to his sense of self-worth. This is also a significant time for building strong moral and ethical values that will stay with your child throughout life.

A child with a loving family, supportive friends and a sense of achievement will have a good self-image. Healthy self-esteem is critical to success both now, at school, and later, at work. Kids who learn to feel good about themselves during the middle years are less likely to grow up into unhappy teenagers—and they're less likely to get mixed up with drugs or other serious problems.

Homework can become a battlefield during these years, and it is almost always an element in any school problem. Specific strategies for coping with homework are covered in Chapter 6. But you cannot apply those strategies without knowing what caused the problem. Otherwise, you will just be trying to correct the symptom. As you'll see in the following cases, you have to commit yourself to effective communication in order to find out what those underlying problems are.

BRIAN: LATE BLOOMER OR FUTURE LOSER?

Brian was never a big reader. His parents and teachers ignored the problem at first. They figured he was just a "late bloomer" and that he'd pick it up when he was ready. He managed to get by in first and second grade, but third grade has been a real struggle. At first, he was trying hard to complete his homework assignments, but now he refuses, saying they're too hard.

His teacher has suggested that he be placed in a special class. Brian feels like a total failure—and his parents are upset and angry that the teacher thinks he is a "slow learner."

Brian's parents finally admitted that their son needed special help. He was evaluated by the school psychologist, who determined that he had a relatively common learning disability— dyslexia, where he tended to reverse letters.

"Why wasn't this recognized sooner?" his parents asked. The reason is that many children with dyslexia get by in the earlier grades because the demands aren't that great. Brian was able to compensate for the problem in those first few years, even though his parents and teachers suspected he was progressing too slowly.

It is harder to cover up a serious reading problem in the middle grades, because the work is more complicated and demanding. Brian never mastered the basic material, so now he's overwhelmed and he's quit trying. Actually, Brian is luckier than some children: eventually, his parents and teachers recognized that there was a reading problem, even if took them a while to realize it. At least they didn't assume that he was refusing to do his homework just because he was bad, or a troublemaker.

Facing the Problem

It is never safe to assume that a child's school problems are simply a phase that he'll grow out of. If your child's development seems out of synch with his classmates, he should be evaluated by an expert. Teachers can usually recognize problems, but they're not always right. When in doubt, get another opinion.

It is too bad that so many parents and teachers miss the early warning signs of learning problems. These problems almost always get worse as time goes on. Without basic skills, the child can't learn more complicated problems. The demands of school work increase, and other students seem to forge ahead. But the learning disabled child gets trapped in a cycle of frustration and failure. He can't "get" the lessons, no matter how hard he tries; the next time, he knows he'll be frustrated and fail, so he may not even try.

Disability Is Not Stupidity

A child with a learning disability will not necessarily tell you he has a problem. He can't tell the teacher, "I can't read this because the letters look blurred," or "I don't hear the difference between the sounds you make in reading," or "The letter 'b' looks just like the letter 'd' to me. All the child knows is that older children in the class are able to do tasks that he can't—and that must mean that he is stupid.

Unfortunately, parents often think that if a child has a learning disability he must be "slow." Therefore, since they know that their child is bright, they don't recognize the problem and look for help early enough. Instead, they tend to wait until the child "catches up" with his classmates. But if there is a learning disability, he will never catch up without help.

Breaking the Frustration/Failure Cycle

Brian belongs in a smaller class where his problem will get special attention. This doesn't mean that he's a "slow learner," as his parents fear. But it will give him the remedial work he needs, with assignments tailored to his abilities. Being given work that he *can* do will help him break out of the cycle of frustration and failure. With this remedial help, he will be able to catch up with his classmates. The chances are excellent that he can go on to a successful school career—including college.

KATY: THE CLASS CLOWN

Katy is a delightful, charming child with a wonderful sense of humor. The problem is, she displays it at the wrong times. The teacher is getting annoyed, because Katy's clowning interrupts her teaching. Whenever Katy's called on, she makes some kind of joke or wisecrack, instead of just answering the question.

Her comedy routines can be irritating to the other children, too: between classes or in the corridors, she's always pulling some kind of prank. The latest one was pouring a container of milk over a boy's head. Katy was sent home with a note from the teacher, complaining about this disruptive and irritating behavior.

"She doesn't know when to stop," her mother told us. "Katy can be funny sometimes, but other times she just goes too far." Katy's mother added, "You know, it's odd—she seems so outgoing, but basically I think she's very shy and insecure."

After talking with Katy and her family for a while, we had to agree: her clowning antics were a way to get attention and instant approval—to make up for her inner feelings of inferiority.

Time for Everyone—Except Katy

Katy is the third of five children in what most people would consider the "perfect" happy family. Her father is a successful businessman, but he also tries to give time to his children. On weekends, especially, he spend hours coaching his two older sons in sports. Katy's mother is an enthusiastic homemaker. She also devotes lots of time to school and neighborhood social activities when she's not occupied with her two toddlers—one's 18 months and the other's three.

But nobody's paying much attention to Katy. She's not neglected, but everyone is so busy with other things, that she's gotten lost in the shuffle. Putting on a show is the best way she knows to get attention—even if it's negative attention.

A Born Comedienne

Katy realized she had a talent for comedy and entertainment when she was only five. Her brothers were four and six years older, so they weren't interested in playing with her. But Katy found out she could get their attention by "performing" for them. Soon, she discovered she could use her silly performances to make other children and adults laugh, too.

But aside from these performances, Katy never learned how to communicate with other people and develop friendships. When the show was over, Katy would withdraw, feeling like she had nothing more to contribute.

The Immediate Problem

Katy must learn to control herself in school. Punishing or nagging won't make her stop: in fact, they could just make her act up even more. The best thing her parents can do is to sit down with Katy and communicate calmly and rationally with her about her behavior. Here's how that conversation might go:

PARENT: Katy, the teacher is upset because your jokes are disrupting the class.

KATY: Everybody laughs. They think it's funny.

PARENT: It's not always funny, is it?

KATY: (Uncomfortable) Maybe not always.

PARENT: I'm sure Bobby didn't think it was funny that you poured milk over his head.

KATY: (Laughing) No, but everyone else did.

PARENT: Sometime people laugh at things that aren't really funny. Lots of time people laugh when someone else is hurt or upset—but that's not really funny is it?

KATY: I guess not if you're the one who got hurt.

PARENT: That's right. And Trisha was hurt because you put shaving cream in her lunch box. You spoiled her lunch.

KATY: It was just a joke.

PARENT: But it wasn't really funny, because it hurt someone.

KATY: I guess I should apologize.

PARENT: I think that Trisha would appreciate that.

Coaching, Not Criticizing

In this exchange, Katy's parents didn't criticize or threaten to punish Katy: *they let her work through the problem by gently leading her to an understanding of why her behavior was wrong. They did not use the conversation to blame her or put her down.*

They can use the same technique to help Katy understand that her wise-cracking in class is also hurtful: it distracts everyone from the lessons, and it's rude to the teacher. *This kind of logic will also help Katy realize that her clowning is never going to win her real friends.*

The Long-Term Problem

Katy won't be able to change her habits overnight. Still, she can be motivated to control herself if she understands how the fooling around hurts her: it keeps her from paying attention to her lessons, annoys the teachers, and puts off the other children. Her parents can help by building up her self-esteem. They have to make time to talk and have fun with Katy, to learn more about her. Her parents need to make time for activities with Katy alone, and to identify her as a person separate from her brother and sister. This will demonstrate that they are interested in her, and that they value other qualities beside her sense of humor.

More Than Just a Clown

Katy doesn't have to totally stop her clowning, but she needs to know that there's a time and a place for her antics—and school is not it. *When Katy believes that she can be loved without having to be a clown, she will be able to control her behavior in school and make lasting friendships—without giving up her sense of humor.*

MICHAEL: WHEN SPORTS STOP BEING FUN

Seventh grader Michael is no more than an average student—except when it comes to sports. His father is constantly bragging about Michael's accomplishments, especially in Little League. He was also a good athlete in school, and spends a lot of time coaching Michael and his teammates. This fall, Michael had his first real disappointment: his father had urged him to sign up for football, but he didn't make first string.

His father complained to the coach and began pressuring Michael to put more into his football. Now Michael has gotten obsessed with football practice—and his father encourages him by spending all his free time coaching him. Michael is neglecting everything else, including his friends and his homework. His primary teacher says that if he doesn't make up the work he's missed soon, he'll be in danger of failing.

Competitive sports can be a very positive influence for a child. They can teach discipline, coordination, self-confidence and team-work. Competitive sports can also have a negative influence. They can make the child feel like a failure, especially when a parent's needs, not the child's, have pushed him into competition too soon.

Living Vicariously

It's easy for parents and children to overemphasize the importance of sports. That's what happened with Michael and his father. His father really enjoys coming home from his high-pressure sales job and unwinding by coaching his son.

There would be no harm in that—except that sports have stopped being fun for Michael. He feels pressured, because he thinks his sports ability is the only thing his father values him for. When he didn't get a good spot on the football team, he felt like he had let his father down.

His father fed these fears, by intervening with the coach and overemphasizing the importance of making the team. He's lost sight of what Michael really needs: a chance to compete at his own level and at his own pace. He's also forgotten that school work and friendships matter as much as—if not more than—sports.

Restoring The Balance

Michael's father has to accept that his son may not be the star player of every sports team. In fact, he doesn't have to be the star of any team. The point of school sports should be fun, as well as self-discipline and competition.

The two of them should decide just how important sports should be in Michael's life. Should it come before homework and friends? Probably not. We suggested that they pick one sport for Michael to concentrate on—baseball would be perfect, since it's played in the summertime. Then, during the school year, Michael can devote as much time to friendships and schoolwork as to athletics.

In the meantime, Michael's father should admit that he overreacted, and let up the pressure on making the first string. Right now, Michael needs to spend some time catching up on the school work he has neglected.

PATRICK: DEFIANT AND DEPRESSED

"When we divorced, we knew it would be hard on the kids," Patrick's mother said. "But we never expected this. Patrick has turned into an absolute monster. He either sulks or storms; whenever you ask him to do anything, he goes into a rage; he's down on everything and everybody. And he refuses to do his homework—because, he says, he doesn't feel like it. Last term, his report card had three D's."

This is a case where the lack of communication between parents and child has created an explosive situation. Patrick's mother says she and her husband "expected" problems when they got divorced. But it doesn't seem like they've done much to prevent them. Emotionally, Patrick is a tinderbox. On the outside, he's angry and defiant. On the inside, he's frightened and depressed.

Divorce: A Stress At Any Age

Divorce is one of the greatest stresses in a child's life, but many parents dismiss how much it affects the child. Especially with an older child, they assume that he'll be unhappy for a while. Then, they reason, he'll get used to it and everything will be back to normal.

There's a major flaw in that reasoning. It's not easy for adults to "get over" a divorce—so why should it be simple for a child?

Ignored Distress Signals

Like many divorcing parents, Patrick's parents got so caught up in their own problems that they ignored his distress signals.

When she thought back, Patrick's mother remembered, "He *was* unusually quiet—almost withdrawn—in the months before

my husband moved out. He was also very obedient and agree-
able about whatever we told him. It was almost as if he thought
he could patch things up by behaving well."

Depression: The Great Masquerader

Patrick reacted to his parents' divorce by getting angry—a
common reaction for a child his age. He's taking his anger out
on everything and everyone around by refusing to do anything
he's asked to do—especially his schoolwork. We explained to
his mother that the best way to help him would be to let him
express his feelings, rather than get into pointless arguments
about his homework.

She soon realized that depression was the real problem hiding
underneath that angry exterior. Once she understood how much
the divorce hurt Patrick, she was able to communicate with him
more effectively. *Instead of getting caught up in fights, they
talked about what was really on his mind.*

In Chapter 2, we talked about how knowing yourself is a vital
part of communicating effectively with your child. "I hadn't
thought much about how my feelings could affect Patrick," his
mother told us later. "I became very depressed and withdrawn
after the divorce. This made Patrick feel doubly rejected and
unloved: his father had moved out physically, and then I shut
him out emotionally." Patrick took his sadness and hurt and
expressed it as anger and aggression. This anger was not directed just at his parents—he turned it toward everything, including
his teachers and his school assignments.

Finding Support

Patrick's mother realized that she would need help providing
Patrick with the support and love he needs. One step she took
was to join a Single Parents' group sponsored by her local PTA.
She's also enlisted her ex-husband's support in providing Patrick
with the extra reassurance and direction he needs now.

Patrick's teachers have also been asked to help—not by
coddling him, but just by being aware of the problem. This
positive attention has helped Patrick feel better about himself
and his parents. He has also learned to separate his distress
about the divorce from the need to keep up with his schoolwork.

QUESTIONS PARENTS ASK

Class Bully

Q. The teacher says our son Benjamin is bullying the other children in his third grade class. He's usually cooperative at home with his older brother and sister, but I have noticed that he can be pretty rough with some of his playmates. We've threatened to punish him if he keeps it up, but nothing we tell him helps. Why does he do this, and how can we stop it?

A. The common wisdom is that children bully each other because they feel insecure. One exception might be in the case of a child with Attention-deficit Hyperactivity Disorder: some "hyperactive" children act aggressively for reasons we don't completely understand. But if ADHD was the cause, Benjamin would probably be difficult and aggressive with everyone, including his brother and sister.

The best advice we can give is to talk with Benjamin. Don't threaten or scold him for being rough or bullying—just ask him why he bosses and hassles other children. Your initial goal should not immediately be to force him to stop, but to discover the cause.

It is quite possible that he is learning bullying and intimidation at home. Take a close, hard look at the way you deal with your children. Do you deal with them fairly and consistently, or do you bully and threaten them into acting as you wish?

The cure is to tell Benjamin—with deeds and words—that bullying will not win friends and earn respect. The message you should send him is that friendship requires giving and taking. If you treat him with love and respect, he'll learn to treat others well, too.

Made-Up Maladies

Q. In the last few months, Alex has been complaining of a lot of headaches and stomach aches, and he's been missing an awful lot of school. Sometimes I wonder if he isn't just making it up, since he tends to get sick on Sunday evenings—but I'm worried that something serious is wrong.

A. It was very observant of you to notice that he tends to get "sick" just before a school day—not on Friday night, when the weekend is ahead! We agree with your suspicion that Alex is "somatic"—that is, he's complaining of physical symptoms to avoid school, whether he's fabricating his illnesses, or really experiencing these symptoms because of his anxiety about school.

Malingering is a common childhood problem, but it's usually not serious. It's best not to give in by letting the child avoid school or doing an unpleasant task because of a made-up ailment.

In Alex's case, you should gently but firmly insist that he go to school, even though he doesn't feel good. Don't berate him for "faking" an illness—this will just make him feel defensive, and he'll insist all the more that he's really sick. And he may really feel sick, even if he isn't actually ill. But getting him to go to school doesn't solve the problem. You still have to find out why he's malingering. Make time to talk over what it is he wants to avoid, and why.

One warning: don't totally dismiss the possibility that something is physically wrong—not all aches and pains are malingering, either. If you suspect a medical problem, have the child examined by a pediatrician.

An Unhealthy Friendship

Q. Our sixth-grader, Carla, is an excellent student, but she's not very attractive and she doesn't have many friends at school. That's why we were so pleased when she made friends with Suzanne, one of the most popular girls in the class. Now we've learned that the teacher suspects Suzanne has been copying Carla's homework assignments.

A. Unfortunately, a girl like Carla can be vulnerable to a social charmer like Suzanne, who has coerced her into doing her work. Carla probably realizes this is wrong, but it's a way to insure the friendship. She also probably understands that this "friend" doesn't really care about her, and that she'll snub her if she doesn't help her cheat.

We don't recommend forbidding Carla from seeing

Suzanne—that usually just makes a child resentful and defiant. But you (and maybe the teacher) should have a serious talk with her about why she is letting Suzanne copy her papers. You should also give Carla some more help with making friends: instead of trying to fit into the "in" crowd, there may be another group of youngsters she would have more in common with. Most important, however, is to improve her self-image. She shouldn't feel she needs to "buy" friendships by letting unscrupulous children exploit her.

Preventing Drinking, Drug Abuse

Q. A group of seventh graders from our local junior high were caught getting drunk at an unsupervised party. Our daughter will start school there in the fall, and we're worried about how to protect her from that kind of bad influence.

A. It's never too early to start educating children about the dangers of alcohol and drug abuse. Many parents deny that these problems could affect their children. But we know from professional experience that children as young as fifth and sixth grade can get mixed up with booze and drugs. Children with family histories of alcohol and drug abuse are even more at risk for developing these problems. Make it very clear to your child that alcohol and drug use are not acceptable.

Luckily, the schools and society at large are becoming more sensitive to the problem. The best prevention is education and example—and preventive education cannot be started too young.

Remember that *your* actions set the most powerful example. Do you "have" to have a couple of drinks (or more) to unwind every evening? Or maybe your idea of a good party is one you can hardly remember in the morning? Children whose parents abuse alcohol or drugs are going to get the message that this is okay. If you think your kids don't know about your drinking or drug-taking, you're the only one who's being fooled. So, if you have a problem with drugs or alcohol, get help—if not for your own sake, then for your kids.

Besides setting a good example, you should educate your child about drugs and alcohol. While your example is important, children are affected by the society at large as well. Unfortunately, kids get a lot of messages that drugs, cigarettes, alcohol and sex are cool. You can't protect your child from all these messages, and you can't counter their influence completely on your own.

Connect with your school, public library and local medical center. They can direct you to prevention programs aimed at the proper age group for your child.

Larry: Friendly But Friendless

Q. Our son Larry is an outgoing and rambunctious fourth grader. The problem is that he can't seem to make friends or concentrate on his schoolwork. The pediatrician and school psychologist say that he has hyperactivity syndrome, and they want to put him on a medication called Ritalin. How likely is to help?

A. It's hard to say exactly in an individual case, but 70 to 80% of hyperactive children respond to medication therapy. The improvement is usually immediate. He should be more able to sit still and concentrate on his work, instead of daydreaming, fidgeting or disrupting the other children in the class.

Also, some children with hyperactivity disorder (or ADHD) have trouble making friends because they tend to be impulsive and aggressive. The medication may help his behavioral problems somewhat, but they're not a substitute for consistent parental discipline and guidance. Your child will still need help learning how to make and keep friends. He'll also need remedial help to catch up with his schoolwork.

CHAPTER 5

THE TEENS: LEARNING TO TAKE CONTROL

WHEN CHARLES Dickens wrote, "It was the best of times, it was the worst of times," he was referring to the era of the French Revolution—but his words could apply to adolescence just as well. The teen years are a roller coaster of emotion and experience. One day, the teen is walking on air; the next, he is plunged into despair.

This age, like the early years and the middle years, has its own set of challenges. Teenagers are betwixt and between. They're leaving childhood behind, but they haven't fully entered adulthood. They feel pushed and pulled between the two. They are being attracted by autonomy and independence. At the same time, they're afraid to give up the security of home and the family.

We talked about the early years as a time when children learn to let go of their parents. In the middle years, they learn to belong to their peer group. In the teens, children fully develop their individual identities. This is when children consolidate and build on the skills they have learned so far, in preparation for adulthood. That's why we call the teens a time when children learn to take control.

Of course, anyone who has lived through adolescence knows that this is not an easy task. It's even more difficult when the normal developmental pressures of growing up are complicated by additional problems: failures at school, conflicts with authority, lack of self-esteem, premature sexual activity, drug and alcohol abuse. These things don't necessarily make it impossible for a child to mature normally, but they certainly make it hard.

A lot of the patterns for teenage problems are established during the child's early and middle years. Because they're usually long-standing, these bad habits are especially hard to correct—and that's true for you as well as your teen. If you and your teen are having problems, you've probably gotten locked into some negative patterns of communication and behavior. The more you repeat these destructive patterns, the more you lose. You communicate less and less effectively, and you undermine the influence and authority you have over your child.

To break out of these traps, you'll have to work hard at communicating effectively with your child. You'll have to be the one who takes the first (and second and even third) steps to reopen communications with your teen.

In this chapter, we give some examples of typical teenage school problems and their solutions. As you'll see, there is a magic formula for breaking through to your teen: communication.

But be forewarned: the principles of effective communication are simple, but applying those principles is hard work. There are three keys:

- Be patient
- Listen carefully
- Decide what really matters

With good communication, you and your teen can work together to solve his problems.

CHRIS: REBEL WITHOUT A CAUSE

Thirteen-year-old Chris is constantly getting into trouble. In his latest escapade, he was caught cutting class. This was only the last offense in a long list of problems, including poor grades because he rarely does his homework assignments. Chris has been put on probation at school, and his parents brought him to us to "straighten him out." His father said, "I have tried everything I can think of to discipline this child," he said. "But no matter what kind of punishment I give, or how much I threaten him, he disobeys."

His mother added, "Chris has been difficult since the day he was born. His first full sentence, when I asked him to bring me something, was, 'No, do it yourself.' It seems that everything we've ever told him to do, he does the opposite. We try to discipline him, but nothing works. Some times we don't even bother to get mad or do anything. If we always reacted, we'd be fighting constantly."

Defiance: Sometimes Normal...

It's natural for children to develop a streak of disobedience and stubbornness. The first signs usually emerge between the ages of one and a half and three, which is where we get the phrase "the Terrible Two's." This is a normal development stage. Telling his parents "no" or refusing to obey helps a child develop a sense of independence. Children also use defiance and disobedience as a way of testing their limits—they want to see just how far they can go. Most of the time, however, children will do as they're told, because they essentially want to please you and win your love.

...And Sometimes Not

It is not normal for a child to be constantly defiant and contrary. Some children, like Chris, seem to have developed a temperamental inclination to oppose parents, teachers, and other adults. When parents or teachers impose irrational authority on such a child, they invariably make it worse.

That's what happened with Chris. His parents are very strict and authoritarian—but only sometimes. Other times, they don't react at all. When they punish him, it's disproportionately harsh and arbitrary.

Inconsistent Discipline

Chris's parents are inconsistent about enforcing rules. For example, there's a rule in Chris's household that he can only watch one hour of television a day, after his homework is done. Chris breaks this rule regularly; he often spends three or four hours in the den in front of the TV without his parents saying anything.

"We can't keep an eye on him every minute," his father says. "Besides, when I get home from work, I want to put my feet up and read the paper, not get into a fight with Chris about whether or not he's watched more than his day's share of TV."

If his parents are not willing to enforce the TV time rule, they should drop it. Having a rule that isn't enforced makes the parents look weak and irrational in Chris' eyes.

Unpredictable Punishment

The other mistake the parents make is giving Chris empty threats. "Usually I can spend the whole night watching TV with no problems. But if Dad has some show *he* wants to see, then watch out."

Chris told us, "Last time he got mad 'cause I didn't want to switch the channel, he said he was going to throw the TV out. Fat chance—then he'd miss his stupid news shows."

When the rules *are* enforced, the punishment is usually far worse than the crime. For example, one night Chris was ten minutes late for dinner, which is at 6:00 sharp every night. The penalty was no dinner for a week, although he was expected to sit at the table while his parents and younger sisters had their food. Not surprisingly, this harsh punishment was not carried out all the way, either. "We had to give in after a couple of days," his mother told us. "We couldn't stand to see him looking so pathetic while we were trying to enjoy our food."

Anger and Resentment

Chris has become resentful and angry about his parents' harsh and inconsistent approach to discipline. "They just get mad when they don't have anything better to do. Most of the time, they don't even know what I'm doing and they don't care. Then other times, they go bananas over nothing. If I'm going to be in trouble for doing nothing, I might as well have fun— chances are they won't catch me anyhow."

A New Approach to Authority

Does this mean that Chris's parents should give up trying to discipline him at all and just let him run wild? Not in the least. They just have to restructure the way in which they communicate with him. Chris's parents have fallen into a destructive trap of imposing their authority and will without clear reasons and without regard for Chris's true needs. Effective, rational authority has to be based on love, fairness, and caring.

Accentuate the Positive

The most constructive thing Chris's parents can do to modify his behavior is to focus on his positive achievements and good behavior. Their pattern so far has been to pay attention only when Chris has misbehaved. In fact, some of Chris's acting out may be an effort to get some kind of attention, even if it is negative. Instead, his parents should make an effort to find things to praise.

It's a well-known principle of psychology that you can encourage children to act as you wish by rewarding positive behavior and simply ignoring negative behavior. Punishing negative behavior may or may not discourage that behavior, but it won't induce your child to act the way you want.

It might not always be easy for Chris and his parents to see eye to eye, but if they are persistent, their communication will improve. As their communication improves, and his parents learn how to treat Chris fairly and rationally, his behavior will also improve. (We talk more about the issue of discipline and authority in Chapter 6.)

NATALIE: DRUGS, SEX AND ROCK 'N ROLL

Natalie is a 16-year-old who was always a good student and a "nice" girl. Her family recently moved to a relatively small Southern town from New York City, when her father changed jobs. "Since we moved, Natalie has undergone a personality change," her mother told us. "She was practically a model child; she was a good student, and she had nice, pleasant friends. She took flute lessons, and she practiced regularly. On

Saturdays, she and her friends were as likely to go to a museum or the library as shopping or the movies.

"I don't know what's happened since we got here," her mother continued. "She's met a crowd of older girls, who frankly, are trash. Instead of hooking up with a nice crowd, Natalie has latched onto these tramps. She's dressing like them, in their sleazy tight pants and short skirts. She's started listening to their crummy rock music, and she hardly practices her flute at all." Natalie's grades are slipping, too. Her homework is suffering because she spends hours on the phone every night.

Moving is hard on children, especially teenagers. In terms of psychological development, this is the time when a teenager's peer group is most important. As they progress through their teens and strengthen their personal identity, adolescents become more self-reliant. In the early teens, however, belonging and being accepted by kids their age is the most important thing.

From an Insider to an Onlooker

Natalie's parents moved just when she had become secure with her outside world. As her mother said, she had a nice group of friends, activities that interested her, and the habit of success and achievement at school. Natalie felt confident and in control. But suddenly all these things were taken away from her, and she was forced into a new environment.

Natalie became an outsider in a place where many of the other children had known each other since kindergarten. She felt threatened and insecure, afraid that the new kids wouldn't like her. In fact, the kids in her new class did snub her—they were just as intimidated and put off by her big-city sophistication as she was made awkward by their small-town cliquishness.

An Instant Identity

That explains why Natalie latched onto the first kid who befriended her: a 17-year-old girl who lived down the street. "She thought it was cool that I came from Manhattan," Natalie said. "Everybody else here is a nerd, but Adrienne and her friends are hip."

When she moved away from her old friends and school,

Natalie felt as if she had lost her identity. But this new group of kids had given her a sense of "instant" identity—all she had to do was dress like them and listen to their music. The question is, is there any harm in that? Are Natalie's parents right to be concerned about her sudden change in tastes? If so, is there anything they can do to steer her back?

Drugs and Sex: Realistic Worries

"We're worried that Natalie's going to blow her chances for college—assuming, of course, that she doesn't get herself into trouble with sex or drugs before then," her mother said. "I heard that one of these girls had an abortion last year. And I suspect some of them smoke pot."

Her father added, "I know it sounds stupid, but I don't like the idea of her listening to music that tells her drugs and sex are okay. How can she resist something everyone around her says is 'cool'? I've got half a mind to forbid her to see these kids, if I thought it would work."

Unfortunately, every parent today has to worry about teenagers getting mixed up with drugs or sex. Our society is filled with messages saying they're okay. Rock n' roll music, especially the "heavy metal" type, contains many explicit messages about drugs and sex. And there are plenty of pressures and stresses that are likely to drive kids to self-destructive behavior. Unhappy, unhealthy children are frequent victims. Healthy kids, however, are not so likely to succumb to these temptations.

Preventing Problems Through Communication

We told Natalie's parents that there wasn't necessarily any harm in what their daughter was doing. Millions of teenagers dress "offensively" and listen to "appalling" music. But those are superficialities. The real issue is, what's going on in your child's mind? Natalie and her parents need to spend time in effective communication. This will give Natalie the chance to be reassured that her parents love and support her, and it will give her parents a chance to get to know her better. Open, effective communication will make it possible for Natalie to develop the inner strength she needs to separate herself from this dead-end crowd.

Trading an Image for Inner Security

After they reestablish rapport with Natalie, her parents can help her find her own identity, so she doesn't need to borrow it from an outside group. The move made her feel uprooted and insecure, so she needs to learn that she can get security from within.

Her parents shouldn't nag, but they should encourage her to get reinvolved with her schoolwork and her music lessons. She will find that she still gets satisfaction from these things—and she may even start relationships with other children who share her interests.

Reestablishing Positive Values

Natalie's father realizes that trying to stop her from hanging around with her "trashy" friends would be pointless and counterproductive. If she's forbidden to see them, Natalie would probably just defy her parents to assert herself. It also won't help if her parents put these friends down and ridicule them. That will make Natalie feel attacked and belittled, since she has identified so closely with them.

Instead, her parents should quietly encourage the values they think are important. If Natalie is given positive support to pursue her other interests, she will drift away from this crowd on her own. Her parents should talk with Natalie's guidance counselor and discuss which activities she should be encouraged to join.

KEITH: THE SON WHO NEVER MEASURED UP

When 17-year-old Keith's parents contacted our office, they were distraught. His grades had gone from bad to worse, and now they had gotten a notice that he had been truant for two days last week. "We just don't understand what went wrong with Keith. His mother and I never had a minute's trouble with his older brother or his younger sister. We've done everything we could to help him succeed, but he's never been willing to make the extra effort."

Lately, Keith has become increasingly hostile and withdrawn from his parents. When he's home, he stays in his room listening to heavy metal groups like Twisted Sister. On weekends, he stays out until midnight and later with an older crowd of "losers." His mother told us, "He's been seeing a girl, but I wouldn't call it dating. They just go to her house, where anything goes—she lives with her divorced mother and the mother's live-in boyfriend."

Keith's parents have good reason to be concerned. The immediate danger is that Keith is giving off a lot of warning signals that he's very unhappy—and that he's probably taking drugs. The warning signs of drug abuse include his hostility and withdrawal, his school failure and truancy, and his association with a crowd of high-school dropouts who don't fit in with anyone but each other. (See the checklist on page 88 for other signs of drug use.)

What Went Wrong?

"We gave Keith all the same advantages as the other two," his mother told us somewhat defensively. "But he never made anything of himself. Michael, who's twenty, is at Brown University on a full scholarship. He's not an academic grind, either; he's also a member of the student council and captain of the tennis team. Susan, who's fourteen, is also an A student, and she's just landed the lead in the class play." Keith's father added, "We're very proud of those two—but Keith's been a real disappointment."

Unfair Expectations

The problem for Keith was that he couldn't measure up to his parents' ambitious expectations. He started out as an average student—not much better and not much worse than the majority of the kids in his class. Still, his parents pushed him to do better, constantly comparing him with his older brother.

He faced the same problem at school, where most of his teachers had taught his smart and charming older brother. When he turned in less than brilliant work, the teachers assumed that he just wasn't trying. Unfortunately, he was, and that was the best he could do. Because of these unrealistic expectations, Keith got trapped into a cycle of failure. Soon he quit trying. After all, he reasoned, if I don't try, then I can't really fail.

Don't Compare—Congratulate

You should never compare one child with another. Different children have different abilities and limitations. Instead of comparing him with his brother and sister, Keith's parents should have just encouraged him to do the best he could. Then they could have congratulated him for the effort, which might have inspired him to try even harder next time.

Keith told us, "In grade school and junior high it was always, 'Michael did this and Michael did that.' Now it's Susan who's the big shot. Everybody keeps comparing me to them. But maybe I don't want to be like them." Keith withdrew and tried not to care in order to save his pride. In the process, he became a very lonely, isolated child.

A Family's Failure

When we talked about these problems with Keith's parents, it was easier for them to understand why Keith had "failed" —actually, they had all failed. They could also see why Keith had taken up with a group of "losers." He was accepted by these kids, who were aimless, drifting dropouts; they were just as lonely and alienated as their son.

Keith shares some of the problems of both cases we discussed earlier. Like Chris, he's fallen into a pattern of defiance and hostility—both to rebel against "authority" and to get attention. And like Natalie, he's sought out an identity by copying the style of a crowd of misfits, who make him feel as if he belongs. The difference is that Keith's problems have gotten serious, and they've been complicated by drug abuse.

A Prescription for Healing

Unfortunately, it will be impossible for Keith and his parents to correct these self-destructive patterns without outside help. Keith may need a brief hospitalization to help him get over his drug problems. Both he and his parents will need psychiatric counseling to help them develop healthier ways of communicating. It's a pity that Keith's childhood has been scarred, but with commitment and love, this family can heal some of its psychological wounds.

QUESTIONS PARENTS ASK

Addiction and Prescription Medication

Q. Our 14-year-old son will be starting ninth grade in the fall. He was diagnosed as having ADHD (Attention-deficit Hyperactivity Disorder) several years ago, and he's been taking Dexedrine with pretty good results. But with everything you hear about drug abuse, I'm afraid he'll take the drug to get "high."

A. Stimulants like Dexedrine can make adults feel "up" or happy, but they don't have this effect on hyperactive children. If anything, your son probably complains that the medication makes him feel too "mellow."

Still, you're wise to be concerned. Even though your son is not likely to try to get high on it, Dexedrine, or "speed," is a commonly abused drug. We'd be most worried that your son's friends might want to abuse his prescription. The best way to control that is to monitor his pill-taking, dispensing only one dose at a time. Also be sure that this medication is reviewed regularly with his physician. If drug abuse does become a problem for a youngster with ADHD, there are alternative medications with no abuse potential.

Improving Grades

Q. Our 15-year-old never manages to get good grades—just C's. I know she could do better if she would just try.

The problem is that she doesn't spend enough time on her homework. She's always promising to do it, as soon as whatever TV show she's watching is over. But there's always another show. I feel like a nag, constantly reminding and lecturing her about how important it is to do homework, but I can't get her to change her habits.

A. You probably already know that your daughter doesn't need another lecture on the value of homework. What she does need is to develop good study habits. This will take some effort, because both you and she have to unlearn bad habits first.

We discuss dealing with homework in more detail in Chapter Seven, but here are some basic guidelines:

1. Don't nag. This feeds bad habits because the child gets as much (or more) attention for bad behavior as good.

2. Don't put too much emphasis on grades. What counts is what the child has learned, not the letter grade. You should be encouraging your daughter to do her best instead of worrying only about her report card.

3. Don't demand perfection—just improvement. Your goals should be realistic, and you should be prepared for occasional backsliding. Failure is not a disaster: it's a problem that can be corrected.

4. Practice problem-solving—not fault-finding. Make it easy for your daughter to do her homework. Agree upon a reasonable time for it to be done. Then make sure she has a quiet, private place in which to work, free from distractions. Offer help and advice only when she asks for it.

Of course, this assumes that your daughter is motivated to get better grades. If she isn't, then maybe the only problem is your expectations. Talk to her and find out what *she* really wants. Maybe academic performance is not important to her, and you're imposing your own values on her. However, *you* are the parent. A reasonable school effort and grades consistent with ability are appropriate expectations for a parent.

Clashing Tastes

Q. Our teenage son is basically a good kid, and he works hard. The only thing that we cannot agree on is his personal appearance. Since he started high school, he never laces up his sneakers, and he always wears the same threadbare jacket. He insists on wearing his hair cut at about four different lengths, from long to short. He looks like a bum who lost a fight with a lawn mower. When I complain, he just shrugs and says, "That's how everyone dresses." I can't believe the school allows the kids to dress like that.

A. There's no point in fighting over something as trivial and superficial as your son's appearance, as long as he's not violating the school's dress code. Be glad that he's a well-adjusted child and doing well at school, and try to not pay too much attention to his punk-hobo fashion style.

PARENTS, BEWARE

So much has been said about how difficult the adolescent years are that you might think that it's normal for a teenager to be depressed or doing badly at school or experimenting with sex or drugs. But it's not true— adolescence is *not* necessarily a deeply troubled time. It is normal for teens to be moody and emotional, but the moods should shift, and the emotions should pass from high to low.

Teens do experience extremes of emotion; they do need to test authority; they will experiment with dangerous behavior. But a teen who is doing any of these things compulsively and destructively is a child who is in pain. Don't ignore the distress signals of problem behavior—get the child help.

Children, especially teenagers, have a right to make personal statements when it comes to tastes in hair, clothes, and music. They should also be allowed to develop their own values in regard to their choice of friends, political beliefs, life goals, and personal habits. If you're lucky, they'll share the values you care about most. In any case, they'll respect your preferences as much as you respect theirs.

By the way, if your son was violating the school dress code, you should let him know that you expect him to abide by the rules. But it would be all right for him to dress the way he wants outside of school. Remember that his wardrobe is going to be most influenced by what the other kids are wearing; teens tend to dress in "uniform."

Remember, there is no point in fighting trivial battles. Instead, pick battles that are worth winning *and* winnable. Also, the object is to win the "war," not every battle.

CHAPTER 6

THE PITFALLS OF PARENTHOOD

IN THIS chapter, we will give you some tips about common parental pitfalls. These are traps that parents can easily stumble into. You may have gotten stuck in one of these areas either because you don't know the facts or you are not sure how you should act:

- how do you walk the line between demanding too much and expecting too little?
- when is a child likely to be over-stressed?
- how can you recognize depression?
- what are the warning signs of drug and alcohol abuse?
- does your child have an absolute right to privacy?
- should you be stricter? or more lenient?

Three words can help you avoid these parental pitfalls: **Trust Your Instincts.**

If you think something is wrong, it probably is: use common sense and effective communication to uncover the true problem and find a workable solution. You should never be passive when it comes to your child's welfare. Fight for what you think is right.

DO YOU EXPECT TOO MUCH—OR TOO LITTLE?

One of the most common traps that parents fall into is the development of unrealistic expectations. Some parents put much too much stress on the external or superficial achievements of their children. Other parents go to the opposite extreme, and don't demand anything from their children in terms of grades, dress or behavior.

Whichever extreme the parents fall into, the child suffers. If you ask too much, he may rebel against your constant demands. But if you ask too little, he will probably achieve even less. Here are some case examples that show what we mean.

From Success to Sudden Failure

Kenny was sent to us when he was a senior in high school. He had been a very bright student—even brilliant—and he had won several science prizes. His parents were hoping that he would get early admission to Stanford University, when suddenly, he started to flunk out. If his parents asked him why he wasn't doing his work, Kenny would give them vague answers. "School's dumb," he would say, or "I don't see the point of college." But what was really going on was that Kenny had finally found a way to control his parents. They had put so much stress on the importance of grades and school that he felt this was the only thing they cared about. As long as he fulfilled his parents' expectations by doing well, Kenny felt they were controlling him. Now, he realized, he could control them (even if negatively) by failing.

Your child needs to know that you love and value him because of who he is—not what he does. You shouldn't make some external achievement—like grades, or sports, or looks—the only goal. If he thinks your acceptance is based on these superficial things, he will feel vulnerable and manipulated. He is also liable to use these goals against you—by failing.

Asking Too Much

When parents demand too much, children may become chronic under-achievers. An average student whose parents nag him constantly about grades may stop trying. As one of our young patients told us, "If I get a C, they want to know why I didn't get a B. So what difference does it make if I get a D? They're going to yell at me in any case." Another student we know is a very talented gymnast, but she refuses to compete. She is so afraid of failing, and disappointing her parents, that she isn't willing to try.

We can also ask too much of our children emotionally and psychologically. When you set tasks or organize activities for your child, always ask yourself, "Is he ready for this?" For example, it may be all right to expect a seven-year-old to help with dinner preparations—but it is not fair to expect him to get the meal ready on his own. Your expectations should match the individual child's capabilities and stage of development.

Asking Too Little

At the other end of the spectrum are the parents whose expectations are too *low*. These are the parents who protect and indulge their children to the point that they are never challenged. But if a child is never challenged, what will motivate him to succeed?

We Can't All Be Superstars, Can We?

"I never asked that much from Jody," her mother told us, "just that she be herself, and have a good time. Life is too short to waste on studying and worrying. Besides, we can't all be superstars." Jody certainly didn't waste any time studying: she failed so many courses last term that she's going to have to repeat tenth grade.

Jody's problem is she doesn't see the point in trying, because she doesn't believe she could succeed. Her parents didn't expect much from her, and she's living up to their expectation.

What will become of Jody if she doesn't get help soon? Chances are good that she will drop out before graduation. She will probably spend her time hanging out with other "losers" —alienated kids who have flunked out, and who don't fit in. Maybe she will start abusing drugs or alcohol to kill the pain and emptiness she feels.

Jody's mother hasn't done her any favors with her "laid back" views. It is true that some parents over-emphasize grades— but every child should be expected to work at school. The basic skills he learns now will determine his future success or failure. Maybe your child will never go to Harvard or MIT, or even to college at all. That's not the point: your goal should be to help your child become the best person he can be.

We're not saying that every child has to be at the top of the class, or the best athlete or the president of the student union. But every child has the right to fulfill his potential. You can help by setting goals that are appropriate to his age and ability. That will teach him the habit of working hard, and succeeding. To set no goals—or impossible ones—will only teach him the habit of failure.

RECOGNIZING STRESS

In Chapter 1, we mentioned that problems can develop when children are placed under stress. Separation is one common kind of stress—separation occurs when a child is left with a baby sitter, or goes to nursery or grade school, or leaves for camp, or goes alone to stay with relatives. A child may also suffer separation stress when parents divorce, if there's a death in the family, or even if a parent goes on a business trip.

School is also a source of stress. The most common school stress is competition—in sports as well as for grades and honors. There is also social stress—to make friends, to fit in, and be popular. In some parts of the country, children may even be physically afraid at school—they may be places where theft and violence occur, especially if drugs are common.

Symptoms of Stress

Like adults, different children can have very different reactions to stress. Sometimes, even negative stress can have a positive effect—the child rises to the challenge of the situation and shows surprising strength. An example might be the thoughtless, absent-minded teenager who starts doing all the housework when his mother gets sick.

But other children, in other situations, may be devastated by stress. For example, a child who was bullied on the way home from school may become terrified to walk that same route alone.

WARNING SIGNS OF STRESS

The most common symptom of stress in children is anxiety. This may be directed at the specific event, or it may just be a general sense of uneasiness. Here is a partial list of some of the physical and psychological symptoms of stress:

- Accident proneness
- Overly susceptible to illness
- Headaches
- Stomach aches
- Sleep problems
- Appetite changes
- Bullying, aggressiveness
- Withdrawal, fearfulness
- Depression
- Lying, Cheating
- Truancy
- Failing Grades
- Drug, alcohol use

Controlling Stress

It may not be possible to eliminate stress from your child's life. But you should be aware of it, and sensitive to how it affects your child. The best defense against stress is understanding. Encourage your child to talk to you about things that worry him. Don't dismiss his fears, but talk through them with him so that he can understand them and control them better.

RECOGNIZING DEPRESSION: A MATTER OF LIFE AND DEATH

Most of us like to think of childhood as a happy time. Unfortunately, life is not always happy. Sad things happen, people get sick and die, parents divorce. We'd like to shield our children from these troubles, but we can't. Sometimes, these painful life events can lead to clinical depression.

Everyone gets depressed from time to time, especially if

something sad or stressful has happened. Children have a right to their moods, and you needn't be too concerned if your child is "down" for a short period of time. But depression can be a very serious illness. A depressed child is at risk for many other problems, from school failure to drug abuse and suicide.

Get professional help if any of the following is true for your child:

- depressed for more than two weeks
- recurring bouts of depression
- severely depressed (to the point of incapacitation or suicide)
- depression with sleep or appetite changes
- depression associated with deterioration in school performance or family functioning.

Subtle Symptoms of Depression

An adult may be able to say, "I feel depressed," but a child, even a teenager, may not realize why it is that he feels badly. Therefore, you have to be alert to the symptoms of depression, and get the child help even if he doesn't ask for it.

The problem is that, depression can be very hard to recognize. Like stress, depression takes different forms in different children. Depression is not always obvious, especially in children. They may or may not simply act sad and mope around. They're also likely to have behavioral problems or physical complaints.

Not all children who are depressed will seem "down" or "blue." In fact, they may become hostile or aggressive. For example, Patrick, the boy we described in Chapter Four, reacted to his parents' divorce by becoming defiant, rejecting everyone and everything around him.

DEPRESSION: SYMPTOM CHECKLIST

If your child has several of the following symptoms for more than a week or two, suspect depression. Depression can be a serious disorder, and the child should be treated by a professional.

- Change in mood:
- Generally unhappy, sad, or "blue"
- Irritable, cranky or erratic behavior
- Lack of pleasure; no longer enjoys favorite things
- Low self-esteem; feelings of guilt; wishes he were dead
- Withdrawal; loneliness
- Decreased concentration
- Poor schoolwork
- Indecisiveness
- Aggressiveness
- Change in energy/activity level (usually slowed down; sometimes, speeded up or "hyperactive")
- Morbid thoughts (obsessed with death, talks about or attempts suicide)
- Physical problems or complaints:
- Sleep disturbances (insomnia *or* sleeping too much)
- Eating habits (overeating *or* loss of appetite)
- Failure to gain weight (young child)
- Various aches and pains
- Easily tired

If your child has more than four of these symptoms for longer than two weeks, have him evaluated by a pediatrician, psychologist or psychiatrist. Depression can be a difficult problem to diagnose in children, so make sure the professional you consult is knowledgeable.

Who Gets Depressed?

Depression can occur in any child, at any age, but certain factors may increase the child's risk:

- Age: depression becomes more common as the child gets older
- Preschool ("Terrible Twos"): Rare
- Early/Middle School ("Sulky Sevens"): Increasingly frequent after age ten
- Junior/Senior High ("Trying Teens"): Suicide a major cause of death
- Sex: in the earlier years, boys are more likely to become

depressed than girls, but later on, girls become more prone
to depression
- Family history: child is more likely to suffer from depres-
sion if parents or other close relatives have been depressed,
suicidal, alcoholic, or in trouble with the law
- Stress: any major stress
- Abuse or neglect
- Physical illness

Causes

Doctors recognize several types of depression. Depressive
reactions and major depressive illness are two of the more
common and important types of depression. Depressive reactions are usually milder, transient, and related to specific stress
or loss.

Depression as part of an adjustment to a life stress is the type
most people are familiar with: this is a reaction to a stress or
situation that is sad, like death, divorce or some other kind of
loss. Such depressions are usually transient— that is, they last
only a few days or weeks. If the symptoms last more than a few
weeks, treatment is needed.

Major, or "endogenous" depression is a serious—though
common and treatable—psychiatric disorder, Endogenous means
"from within," and it indicates a kind of depression that is
related to a chemical imbalance in the brain. This type of
depression should be treated by a psychiatrist: there are several
very helpful medications, which can be used in children as well
as adults. Often a major depression can be triggered by a stress
or loss in a susceptible child (a child who is predisposed to
developing depression because of a chemical imbalance that can
be inherited).

SUICIDE FACTS AND WARNING SIGNS

- Suicide is the third leading cause of death among high
school students.
- Girls attempt suicide more often than boys; but boys

who try to kill themselves are more likely to be successful than girls.

- Girls are more likely to talk about suicide and show open signs of depression that boys, who tend to hide or suppress their feelings.
- Every year, two million teenagers (age 15 to 19) attempt suicide. Ninety percent of these attempts are made by girls.
- 5,000 teens actually kill themselves every year. 70% of the "successful" suicides are boys.

Not all suicidal children are depressed, but the child who is chronically depressed is the greatest risk. Watch for any of the following signs:

- Talks (or even hints) about suicide
- Depression or withdrawal
- Obsessive or morbid fascination with death, dying, or violent movies
- Poor self image
- Excessive feelings of guilt
- Death or suicide of friend or classmate
- Gives away a prized possession
- Heavy involvement with drugs or alcohol
- Reckless, dangerous behavior

RECOGNIZING DRUG ABUSE

There's been a lot of publicity about the Federal Government's "Just Say No" campaign against drug use. And after many years of rising drug use, it appears that the anti-drug educational programs may be working. For the first time in a decade, the extensive survey of the High School Seniors conducted by the University of Michigan and National Institute of Drug Abuse indicated in 1987 that some indications of drug use had decreased. But the sad fact is that drug use by school children remains a problem: 57% of the 1987 senior class had tried an illicit drug. Drug and alcohol use can be a major cause of school, behavior, and learning problems. Here is just a few of the more sobering statistics:

- 90% of all high school graduates have smoked marijuana at least once.
- 60% smoked their first joint between 6th and 9th grade.
- 15% of high school seniors have used cocaine.

When it comes to drugs, many kids claim they can "take them or leave them"—and maybe you want to believe that. Maybe you even think, "A little pot never killed anyone. It's okay for kids to experiment."

The truth is, street drugs are more powerful and addictive than ever before. Add to that the fact that street drugs may be adulterated with toxic poisons, and it's clear that the "experimenting" child has embarked on a deadly adventure. Marijuana alone probably never did kill anyone, but pot laced with "Angel Dust" can be lethal. Experimenting with drugs is like playing Russian roulette. Alcohol and marijuana can be "gateway" drugs to "harder" drugs, like cocaine and heroin. And we have observed that more and more teenagers are starting their drug use with cocaine. Crack, a very dangerous, smokeable, and initially affordable, form of cocaine, is surprisingly available in many schoolyards.

Even if there are no immediate physical repercussions, the emotional and intellectual price of drugs is high. The child may start off experimenting, but before long, he's seduced into the dream-like, pain-free world of drugs, where grades, teachers, and parental nagging can't touch him. He's robbed of his childhood and of the opportunity to grow, and he's too dulled by the drugs to learn.

The child taking drugs is also more likely to be depressed—it's hard to say whether the depression leads to drug-taking, or drug-taking leads to depression. In any case, the child becomes caught in a vicious cycle, with no apparent way out.

If you suspect your child is taking drugs, **don't turn your back. Get him help.**

Is Your Child Taking Drugs?

Drug addiction is subtle and insidious. Kids don't believe it can happen to them, and parents think the only drug addicts are the typical street-corner "junkies." But addiction doesn't have to be obvious. The following are some of the subtle signs that your teenager might be hooked; but remember there is no single telltale sign of alcohol and drug abuse. A pattern of unexplained deterioration in a number of areas, including school performance, is probably the best alarm.

Physical

- Loss of appetite
- Dilated pupils or red eyes
- Sniffling, runny nose

Emotional/Mental

- Withdrawn from family, friends
- Inability to have "fun"
- Few hobbies or interests
- Unkempt, neglects appearance
- Lethargy ("nodding out")
- Loss of memory
- Hostile
- Drop in grades

Behavioral

- Erratic, irritable behavior
- Unexplained change in activities
- Sudden change of friends
- Irresponsible
- Dishonest or manipulative with others
- Truancy

Other

- Your money or valuables "disappear"
- Chronic lying
- Physical evidence of drugs, drug paraphernalia

PREVENTING DRUG AND ALCOHOL ABUSE

With drinking and drugs so common in our schools, how can you protect your child from them? Your best tactic is through open and effective communication. We talk about some specific case examples in Chapters 4 and 5, but we should repeat that advice here:

First, be honest with yourself. Don't deny the possibility that your child could get mixed up with drugs or alcohol. Any child is vulnerable, and it's never too soon to start preventive education.

Second, be honest with your child. What kind of example do you set? Do you drink too much? Are you dependent on drugs, whether illegal street drugs or tranquilizers, barbiturates or amphetamines "prescribed" by a doctor? If the answer is yes, then you will have a hard time convincing your child that he should abstain.

Remember, children *are* under powerful pressure from their peers.

Thankfully it is the parents who instill—and enforce—deep, lasting values. Strong values, a good self-image, and the security of your love will give your child the strength to resist the temptations of drugs.

THE RIGHT TO PRIVACY vs YOUR NEED TO KNOW

Parents of troubled children, especially kids with drug problems, often tell us that they're afraid of prying too closely into their children's affairs. One mother admitted to us that she could smell the pot her daughter was smoking in her bedroom for months before she confronted the 14-year-old girl. "I had to respect her right to privacy, didn't I?" she asked us when her daughter was brought to the hospital after taking an "accidental" overdose of barbiturates.

The answer is NO. Your child's right to privacy is never as important as his right to a healthy, normal childhood. Drugs rob him of that opportunity. You have a right, and even a need to know if your child is mixed up in something that could be harmful. Unfortunately, parents sometimes want to ignore or deny their children's problems. Maybe they're embarrassed by them, or hope they will go away on their own.

Don't Ignore—Confront

Instead of ignoring problems, confront yourself and your child with them. We don't mean to confront them in a hostile, belligerent way. Instead, take your questions and concerns to the child, and present them in a caring, loving way. As an example, here's how one father we know approached his sixteen-year-old daughter when he suspected that she was taking drugs:

> FATHER: I've been worried about you—you don't seem yourself lately. I'm afraid you've been taking drugs.
> DAUGHTER: That's ridiculous.
> FATHER: I hope I'm wrong—but you seem to be sending out a lot of signals, and you've been withdrawn and short-tempered.
> DAUGHTER: I am not, it's just that you're too picky.
> FATHER: I'm sorry you feel that way, and I'd like to talk to you about it. But first, I'd like to look through your room for drugs—would you like to stay with me while I do?

Not surprisingly, the teen went storming out of the house after this exchange—but she respected the way her father treated her. He was open and honest about his concerns, but he didn't falsely accuse her without the facts. He searched her room, but he did it openly, so she didn't feel spied on, or like her privacy was "violated." The message she got was "I'm worried about you," not "I don't trust you."

In some situations, if drug use is suspected, a blood or urine drug screen should be performed to help answer that question. Your pediatrician, psychiatrist, or other therapist can help you arrange testing if needed.

AUTHORITY AND DISCIPLINE

Many parents wonder either "Am I too strict?" or "Am I too indulgent?" But whether you're very lenient, or not at all lenient, almost all parents agree that children need *some* discipline. The question really should be what *kind* of discipline, rather than how much.

In thinking about the role of discipline and authority in raising your child, it helps to think about the different ways these two words can be defined. Each has a positive meaning as well as a negative one:

Discipline

POSITIVE—Verb: to train or develop; to correct or mold behavior, mental abilities and moral character. Noun: a set of rules or methods; orderly conduct or behavior. Related word: disciple; one who accepts the teachings of a master and assists in spreading them, an active adherent. Synonym: self-control.

NEGATIVE—Verb: to punish or penalize; submit to rules and authority. Noun: punishment, control. Related word: disciplinarian; one who enforces or believes in strict discipline. Synonym: adversity.

Authority

POSITIVE—Noun: expertise, experience, competence; ability to influence; an expert. Related word: authoritative; having expert knowledge, entitled to obedience or acceptance. Synonym: influence.

NEGATIVE—Noun: power to command or enforce; a person with power to command. Related word: authoritarian; favoring absolute or blind obedience to authority. Synonym: power.

Be Authoritative, Not Authoritarian

Our children need discipline and authority in the positive sense. We should be their mentors and teachers, not rigid power figures who impose arbitrary rules. There is a very practical reason for this: using power to control your children does not work. Using influence and respect does.

It is relatively easy to coerce a young child into obeying you—adults have a great deal of authority and power over young children. A ten-year-old can easily be influenced by a system of rewards and punishments. For example, if he does his homework, he can watch TV; or if he rakes the leaves, you will give him five dollars for the movies.

But as your children grow up, your power diminishes. Children realize that their parents are not the all-powerful, all-knowing beings they once thought. Also, as they become more independent, you start to run out of effective rewards and punishments.

Teenagers can be especially resistant and rebellious when you threaten to punish them. If you tell your teenage son that he can't watch TV until his homework's done, he's likely to sulk off to his room—or storm out of the house. All you've accomplished is to start off a cycle of bickering and resentment.

Punishment vs Self-Control

Discipline that is based on self-control is much more effective than discipline based on coercion. If you are a strict disciplinarian, you will probably be able to coerce your children to behave as you want—at least until they are older. But disciplinarians rarely turn their children into disciples.

Power vs Influence

By the same logic, authority based on influence and respect is more valuable than authority based on power. If you're authoritarian, you may be able to control your child's behavior, but you won't necessarily have true authority over him. You must learn to motivate and influence your child to be responsible, considerate, and cooperative. No one else can do the job for you.

Be Fair, Be Consistent, and Set Priorities

In order to discipline effectively and wield positive authority, you must be consistent and fair. If you say no, mean it. Otherwise, your child will constantly be pushing to see if he can change your mind—like last time. And be fair, or the child will lose respect for you. "Forgetting" to bring assignments home for two days in a row may merit a half-hour blackout of a favorite TV program. But it wouldn't be fair to ground the child for a week.

Finally, you must set priorities—some things are important, while others don't really matter. Pick your battles wisely. Don't wear yourself and your child down by arguing over trivial things, like whether your daughter can wear nail polish or your son can wear torn jeans. Save your energy for the important issues, and fight for what's right.

CHAPTER 7

HOW CAN PARENTS HELP?

Throughout this book we have given many examples of what you probably already know: nagging, punishing, and threatening are not effective ways of controlling your child's behavior.

What then, *can* you do that will have a positive effect? We have ten "commandments" for coping with your child's problems.

THE "TEN COMMANDMENTS" OF GOOD PARENTING

1. Improve your communication skills.
2. Control your anger.
3. Be a problem-solver, not a fault-finder.
4. Negotiate agreements.
5. Create a consistent, structured environment.
6. Present a united front.
7. Encourage, don't overwhelm.
8. End homework hassles.
9. Collaborate with the school.
10. Assert your influence.

By applying these principles—and avoiding the parental pitfalls we described in Chapter Six—you will be able to help your child achieve his potential.

1. IMPROVE YOUR COMMUNICATION SKILLS

In Chapter Two, we talked about how communication is the key to helping your child overcome school problems. Learning to be a good communicator requires patience and insight, as well as a genuine desire to communicate. An excellent system for developing your child-parent communication skills is outlined by Dr. Thomas Gordon in his Parent Effectiveness Training (P.E.T.) and Teacher Effectiveness Training (T.E.T.) books and seminars. We can't summarize all his advice here, but we'd like to highlight a few of his key observations.

Roadblocks to Communication

Dr. Gordon has found that when a child comes to his parents with a problem, they tend to respond with one of twelve "roadblocks" to communication. In his book *P.E.T. in Action*, Dr. Gordon gives examples of each of the "roadblock" responses to a 14-year-old boy's statement that he hates homework and school and that he's going to drop out as soon as he's old enough.

1. Ordering, directing, demanding: "No son of mine is going to quit school. I won't allow it."
2. Warning, threatening: "Quit school and you'll get no financial help from me."
3. Moralizing, preaching: "Learning is the most rewarding experience anyone can have."
4. Advising, giving solutions: "Why don't you make a schedule for yourself to do your homework?"
5. Lecturing, teaching, giving facts: "A college graduate earns over 50 percent more than a high school graduate."
6. Judging, blaming, criticizing: "You're being shortsighted and your thinking shows immaturity."
7. Praising, buttering up: "You've always been a good student with lots of potential."
8. Name-calling, ridiculing: "You're talking like a 'hippie.' "
9. Interpreting, analyzing: "You don't like school because you're afraid to put out the effort."
10. Reassuring, sympathizing: "I know how you feel, but school will be better your senior year."

11. Probing, questioning, interrogating: "What would you do without an education? How would you make a living?"
12. Withdrawing, diverting, distracting: "No problems at the dinner table. How's basketball these days?"

Many of these responses are well-intentioned. Nevertheless, the immediate effect they have is to block any further communication from the child. You may feel like you have gotten through to your child, but saying what's on your mind doesn't necessarily address what's on your child's mind. Your child is likely to withdraw or even become angry or resentful when you respond with a "roadblock," because he feels like you're not listening or don't "understand" him.

Before you can help your child solve his problem, you have to understand what the problem really is—not what you assume it is. That means *listening*—not interrogating, preaching, or ignoring. Instead, you should listen carefully to the child's problem, determine what kind of help it is he wants and needs, and then work together to a solution.

The Four Basic Listening Skills

Dr. Gordon identifies four basic listening skills:

Passive listening (silence). Often parents think they're "communicating" when they're the ones doing most of the talking! Let your child do the talking, while you listen.

Acknowledgment responses. Even when you're listening passively, it's helpful to send short signals that let the child know you're paying attention. Acknowledgment responses can be verbal (like "Oh?" "I see," or "uh-huh") or nonverbal (nodding, leaning forward, smiling, frowning).

Door openers (invitations). These are open-ended, nonjudgmental phrases that encourage the child to talk about his feelings or problems. Some effective door openers are, "Would you like to talk about...?" or "I'm interested in how you feel about...."

Active listening. Active listening involves rewording and feeding back what your child tells you. You don't interpret or insert your own message, you just restate what you heard the child say. It goes a step beyond passive listening, because it proves to your child that you truly *understood* what he said. Here are two examples:

> CHILD: I hate arithmetic. It's too hard.
> PARENT: You don't like it because you have trouble understanding it.
> CHILD: Yeah. I'm too dumb to understand it.
> PARENT: You worry that you'll never figure it out.

> CHILD *(in tears):* I fell and scraped my elbow.
> PARENT: It hurts a lot when you get scraped.
> CHILD: No, it doesn't hurt so bad—but it's bleeding.
> PARENT: Seeing all that blood must be scary.
> CHILD: Yeah—I could bleed to death.

One of the advantages of active listening, besides letting your child know that you are listening, is that it helps you make sure that you did understand the underlying message. It also gives you a chance to reword his statement positively, to pave the way to working out a solution.

I-Messages and You-Messages

Dr. Gordon talks about two kinds of "messages" we send to our children about their behavior. "I-messages" describe how we feel about something the child is doing or not doing. "You-messages," on the other hand, are generally orders or criticisms of the child. When our children behave in ways that we find unacceptable, Dr. Gordon points out that "I-messages" are more likely to succeed in getting through than "you-messages."

We can illustrate the difference with an example of what you might say to a 12-year-old who won't do her homework:

You-message: "If you don't do your homework you're going to flunk out."

I-message: "I'm worried that if you don't do your homework, you're going to fall behind your classmates."

The "you-message" is threatening and critical; its hidden content is that the child is lazy and stupid. The "I-message" is supportive and nonjudgmental; the hidden content is simply that you are concerned about her welfare. Because the "I-message" doesn't make the child feel threatened, it opens the door to further communication and problem-solving.

2. CONTROL YOUR ANGER

If your child is having problems in school, you are probably no stranger to feelings of anger and resentment. But getting mad and venting these feelings doesn't help you or your child. How can you cope with these negative emotions?

Retreat

The first thing you should do when you feel yourself losing your temper is to retreat. If you're very angry, you probably won't be able to be fair or deal with your child effectively. It's better to let your spouse deal with the child at these times.

Reflect

The next step is to try to understand the reasons for your anger. Your anger is probably masking another feeling—usually fear or disappointment.

Fear

Anger is often a response to fear. For example, if your child got home two hours late, you'd be rightfully worried about his physical safety. You might yell and get angry, but your underlying emotion would be fear. There may not be any physical danger when your child is having trouble at school, but you can still be afraid of the consequences of his behavior.

Bad grades and a poor education may lead to a low-paying, dead-end job. Petty crime and delinquency now could lead your child into serious trouble with the law when he's older. Getting mixed up with drugs or alcohol and sex can cause real harm to health and safety—and they can also stunt your child's emotional development.

Disappointment

Anger also commonly masks feelings of disappointment, frustration, and embarrassment. We know one father who got furious with his son when he didn't make varsity soccer. The anger was hiding his true feelings of disappointment; everyone in the father's family had excelled at sports, and he found it hard to accept that his son wasn't a "jock," too. You have to determine whether your expectations are realistic, or if you're asking too much from your child.

Frustration

In another family, both parents were university professors with Ph.D.'s. When their daughter was diagnosed as having a learning disability, their first reaction was anger with the school. "We were sure that the school was to blame. Either their diagnosis was wrong, or they were at fault for not teaching her properly. In time, we came to accept her limitations and to realize that our anger was just misplaced frustration and disappointment."

Embarrassment

We can also be embarrassed by our children's bad behavior. We think that if our children fail or get into trouble, somehow this reflects poorly on us. Try to keep your perspective. Instead of worrying about how things "look," concentrate on trying to help your child through his problems. It may also help you to keep in mind that your feelings are shared by all parents whose children are going through hard times.

Depression

People are often surprised to hear that anger can be a symptom of depression. We're all vulnerable to depression from time to time, and this is especially likely when you have to deal with the stresses posed by your child's problems in school. However, you should be alert to the difference between feeling "blue" or "down" in reaction to a specific event, and being chronically depressed. If that's the case, you should get help for yourself—don't take it out on your child.

Reach Out

It often helps to talk to someone—your spouse, a close friend, or a counselor—about angry feelings. This can help you see your problems in a more objective light. Once you understand your feelings, it will be easier to manage them.

An added benefit of understanding the feelings behind your anger can be better cooperation from your child. You may find that if you explain to your child what your real fears are, he'll be more inclined to modify his behavior. It may not always seem that way, but our children want our acceptance and approval. Sometimes they just need to be shown how to earn it.

3. BE A PROBLEM-SOLVER, NOT A FAULT-FINDER

When your child gets in trouble, help him out! Don't waste time or frustrate him with lectures, criticism, or blame. Helping does not mean that you should solve his problems for him. But you should not ignore your child's problems and leave him to try to solve them on his own, either.

You and your child must work to solve problems together. If you impose a solution, one of two things will happen. He'll ignore you and go on doing whatever he was doing wrong. Or he'll count on you to solve his problems for him and never learn to help himself.

Dr. Gordon recommends a "No Lose" method of problem solving. In his book *P.E.T. in Action,* he describes this as a method of resolving conflicts between parents and children, but it can be applied to your child's school problems just as well. The theory is quite simple: the parent and child work together to find a mutually acceptable solution, then decide on a plan to carry it out. No coercion or power is used, and both sides "win" the battle. Dr. Gordon breaks No Lose problem-solving down into a six-step process:

1. Define the problem
2. Generate possible solutions
3. Evaluate the possible solutions
4. Decide on the best solution

5. Implement the solution
6. Follow-up evaluation

PREVENTIVE PROBLEM-SOLVING

If your child keeps getting into the same kind of trouble over and over again, then your problem-solving will have to include problem prevention. In other words, don't give problems a chance to develop.

For example, if your child has been cutting classes, give him a card that each teacher signs at the end of class, so you can be sure he was there. Another example is a child who steals. He may tell you that some new toy or piece of clothing was a "gift" or that he "found" it. You can make it a rule that such objects are not allowed, and if found, you should assume that they were stolen. It is perfectly reasonable to subject the child's room to periodic searches in these circumstances. The same holds true if you suspect your child is drinking or taking drugs.

Preventing your child from harming himself is not an invasion of his privacy. It is a protection of his right to a normal childhood.

---

4. NEGOTIATE AGREEMENTS

This is an extension of the third principle, to be a problem-solver. Once you and your child have agreed on a solution to the problem, negotiate an agreement. If the child is old enough, put it in writing, like a contract.

The most important rule of negotiation is that each side has to give something valuable to the other. That does not mean that you should reward your child with toys or clothes or money every time he does something you want (or does not do something negative). "Giving" can also mean freedom, or attention, or your time.

For example, let's assume that the problem is your child's disruptive classroom behavior. The teacher has reported that instead of just answering questions in class, your daughter is constantly making wisecracks that break up the class. You might negotiate an agreement like the following:

PROBLEM: Wisecracks disrupt class, annoy teacher
DAUGHTER AGREES TO:
• Answer questions straight, with no jokes.
• Speak only when called on by teacher.

PARENTS AGREE TO:
• Let daughter relate the wisecracks she thought of, but didn't make in class, at the dinner table.
• Ask the teacher to reevaluate her behavior in a month, so she does not get unfairly labeled as a troublemaker.

An agreement like this is much more effective than giving your daughter an ultimatum such as "If you don't learn to keep your mouth shut in class, you're going to be sorry." The agreement addresses the specific problem behavior without suggesting that your daughter is "bad." Your side of the agreement supports her in changing her behavior—and you may get an unexpected payoff when you discover that your daughter has a good sense of humor.

(For an example of a homework contract, see the case discussion of "Thomas" at the end of this chapter.)

5. CREATE A CONSISTENT, STRUCTURED ENVIRONMENT

Children need structure and consistency in order to develop the habits and skills that allow them to succeed at school. Make sure that they have a regular schedule for waking up and going to bed, meals, homework, and play. It is unreasonable to expect children to impose a lot of discipline on themselves: a 6-year-old shouldn't be expected to know when to get up to be on time for kindergarten; and it's not fair to expect a 10-year-old to budget time for homework and play without your guidance. A teenager may have more self-discipline, but even so needs structure.

Establish Time to Talk

One of the most effective ways of creating structure in the home is to establish regular mealtimes. A family supper (with no TV!) may seem quaint and old-fashioned, but it's a wonderful way to ensure open communications. Even if it's only a twenty-minute meal of coldcuts or leftovers, the nightly supper provides a forum for talking through problems, hopes, and fears.

If it's absolutely impossible to organize everyone to sit down to dinner together in the evenings, set some other time of day when you can all be together, with the television turned off. This could be fifteen minutes in the morning before everyone goes to work and school, or it could be just before bedtime. Use this time to talk, not bicker and fight. It's a small-time investment for the payoff in how much better you'll know each other.

Be Consistent

Whatever rules and discipline you impose should be consistent. If the rule is "no television before homework," enforce it. Rules should be fair and reasonable—and they are *not* made to be broken. Of course, there will be times when you must suspend the rules, but those times should be exceptions. For example, if your child is supposed to study between 4:00 and 5:30 p.m., but has band practice until 5:00 p.m. twice a week, change the homework hour.

Make Rules Easy to Follow

Create an environment that encourages your child to be disciplined. Don't expect him to concentrate on homework in a noisy room, where the TV is on or someone is talking on the phone.

Encourage Organization

Even if your child has to share a room or work area with you or another child, give him his own area in the room for books, toys, and so on. He should be responsible for keeping this area neat. You can help by making sure there are boxes, shelves, pegs, and hangers, so that everything can be put away easily.

If you expect your child to do chores, have him keep a checklist to make it easy to remember what needs to be done: for example, daily tasks like make school lunch, put schoolbag by front door, lay out clothes for morning, etc., or weekly jobs like rake the leaves or tie up newspapers for recycling. Task checklists are especially helpful for children with Attention-deficit Hyperactivity Disorder and others who are disorganized and forgetful.

6. PRESENT A UNITED FRONT

A corollary to the previous rule, creating a consistent and structured environment, is that you and your spouse must present a solid, united front to the child. In other words, you must agree on the goals you set, you must subscribe to the same values, and both of you must enforce rules and uphold values consistently. If your child gets mixed signals from you and your spouse, he's likely to respond to the most convenient instructions. Or maybe he'll just do his own thing, figuring that since the two of you don't agree with each other, there's no reason for him to go along with either of you.

Agreeing to Disagree (In Private)

It can be hard to agree about everything. Chances are you and your spouse have some genuine differences of opinion about certain aspects of child rearing. Maybe you think mascara is okay on a 16-year-old girl, but your husband thinks it's "cheap." Try to resolve your disagreements in private and negotiate an agreement with each other, in the same way as you would with your child. For example, you might agree that your daughter can wear a little mascara for dress-up occasions, but not to school or when she's wearing jeans. Then both stick with the agreement.

Different Perceptions

Keep in mind that you and your spouse may have different

perceptions and expectations. One parent may be more tolerant than the other. For example, a father may see his son's noisy and messy war games as "macho" and acceptable, while the mother thinks his behavior is obnoxious and disruptive. By contrast, another father might seem too harsh and demanding because he wants no noise or mess when he gets home from a hard day of work. His wife, however, might feel that the disorder is just normal "boy stuff."

Another thing to remember is that your child may act one way toward you and another toward your spouse. Typically, most children are better behaved with their fathers. Try to keep your perspective and avoid the temptation to assume that you (or your spouse) just aren't able to control your child.

Agreement Between Divorced Parents

Divorced parents have special problems in this area. But even they can agree on rules and values that will be enforced, whoever the child is staying with at the time. You two may not care for each other any longer, but you both still care for your child. Keep the child in mind, and don't turn the child's behavior and problems into a battleground for your personal differences. Communicate with each other about problems and potential solutions. Most important, don't undermine each other's authority by allowing the child to "get away with" something the other parent disapproves of.

Preserving Your Relationship

You and your spouse need to communicate about your child's problems—but try not to let these problems spill over into your relationship with your spouse. If possible, plan some time alone together where you don't talk about problems with the child. Plan some activity—hiking, a movie, bowling, whatever—that will force you think about something else. A little time out to yourselves will actually make you more effective in coping with your child's troubles later.

7. ENCOURAGE, DON'T OVERWHELM

Challenge your child enough to give him a sense of accomplishment, but don't discourage him by giving him a task he will fail. If he does fail, don't blame and criticize him. He feels bad enough already. Instead, motivate him to try again, by making it safe for him to risk another failure.

Boost his self-esteem with regular doses of realistic praise and encourage him to undertake activities in which he excels, such as sports, music, art. A child who develops the habit of succeeding in one area will find it easier to take risks and work harder in another area where he has failed in the past.

Don't demand perfection: reward your child for making an effort. You should praise him when he gets a C instead of a D in math, rather than asking why he didn't do better and get a B. Remember, you don't have to limit your praise to school-related activities; you can thank him for doing household chores, walking the neighbor's dog, or babysitting a younger child. The point is just to let your child know you're proud of him, and encourage him to keep trying.

8. END HOMEWORK HASSLES

Homework is probably the universal parent-child battle-ground. It's a rare family where parents and kids don't hassle over homework. If they don't, it's usually because the parents have given up. Don't quit! You *can* help your child to succeed in school, and it's important that you keep trying. You can be open to negotiating just about any other aspect of your child's life, from curfews to clothes, but when it comes to homework, there's only one position. It must get done.

You should not fight with your children about homework, but you should not let them win the homework war either. The basic skills a child learns in school are what will determine how far he can go as an adult. Don't let your child start off with a handicap. Let him know that you expect him to do his homework, and then make sure he gets it done. We go over specific homework tips and talk about a typical case history at the end of this chapter. But here are a few principles you should keep in mind:

- Besides improving grades, working hard and mastering assignments gives a child a sense of accomplishment.
- Children with poor study habits are likely to be labeled as lazy or stupid, leading to a cycle of failure and frustration.
- Good homework habits can be taught at any age, although it's easier to start young.
- Let your child know that homework matters, and that you are confident that he can succeed.
- You don't need to be rich or well-educated to teach your child the value of a good education.
- Homework is the child's personal responsibility—just as a paid job is to an adult.

9. COLLABORATE WITH THE SCHOOL

The school and teachers are your most important allies in solving your child's school problems. Don't wait for the teacher to call you and tell you there's a problem. Make an effort to meet with your child's teachers on a regular basis, so that problems can be prevented instead of corrected. Take the initiative to schedule a conference if necessary, especially in the older grades, when teachers are less likely to request meetings.

Sometimes you may feel at odds with the teacher or the school—you may even feel like they're the reason your child is having difficulties. Try to keep your sense of perspective, and remember that they have their problems and concerns too. If you or your child really dislikes a teacher, examine your feelings before you fly off the handle. Try not to take sides, but don't ignore the situation or blame the child either. See if you can work out a solution with the teacher before taking your problem to the principal.

Whatever your opinion of the teacher, don't criticize the teacher or the assignments in front of your child. Have you ever said that one of your child's assignments was stupid and boring, or that the teacher didn't know anything? These are messages that school does not need to be taken seriously. (See Chapter Eight for more information on school strategies.)

10. ASSERT YOUR INFLUENCE

The final "commandment" for helping your child with school problems is to assert your authority and know when to say "no." This is true for all social and behavioral problems, not just homework.

You're probably thinking, "But that contradicts everything you said about negotiating and listening and not nagging and lecturing!" Actually, it does not. What we're saying is be fair, but be firm. Don't give up, but don't lose your temper, either.

Never threaten your child with punishments you aren't going to carry out, or punish him unfairly. This will just make him lose respect and rebel against you.

Make rules, but make them reasonable, not authoritarian. Make them enforceable, and then enforce them. Your rules should reflect your personal morals and values, and you should set an example of conduct that you want your children to follow. You have to earn your child's respect—you can't intimidate him into accepting your values.

THOMAS: A CASE STUDY OF A HOMEWORK BATTLE

"Homework has become a battleground," Thomas's parents moan. "Most days, he forgets to bring his assignments home. If he remembers them, he puts off starting work for as long as possible."

They nag and threaten Thomas every night after dinner to do his homework. "Eventually, he sits at the dining room table with his assignments. But he's in and out of his seat like a jack-in-the-box, running into the living room to see what's happening on TV. He can't seem to discipline himself, and nothing we say or do makes a difference. If we tell him no TV until his work is done, he just gets mad and refuses to do his work at all."

Almost all parents and children have at least a few homework skirmishes, but for some, it turns into a constant battle. That is what has happened with Thomas. He's in fifth grade now, and he hasn't developed good study habits. His assignments are messy and incomplete, and his report cards are getting worse and worse.

Thomas does not have any signs of a learning disability—in fact, he recently scored very well on a scholastic aptitude test. He is simply not motivated; the teacher says that he's an underachiever. Without the practice that comes from doing homework assignments, Thomas will start falling behind.

The Daily Schedule

Most children need to have a specific time scheduled to do their homework, or they'll never get around to it. There were no rules about homework hours in Thomas's family, and he wasn't about to create his own. In fact, his daily routine conspired against his doing homework.

Thomas didn't want to do his work right after school, because that's when he would play with his friends. At dinnertime, he was expected to set and then clear the table. When the dishes were done, the family would settle down to watch TV.

After his favorite show was over, his parents would start nagging, cajoling, or threatening him to go and do his homework. He'd spend the rest of the evening running back and forth between the dining room where he was working and the living room, where the family was watching TV.

Building Self-Discipline

This is a straightforward problem: Thomas simply needs more structure and discipline to get his work done. That does not mean that his parents should nag or criticize or punish him. They've tried all those things—and learned that they don't work.

Instead of fault-finding, Thomas needs structure and discipline to be motivated. The motivation will have to come from within himself, not his parents. But his parents can help him get organized so that he can succeed.

Thomas's Responsibility

Thomas may not be very interested in doing his homework—but he has to do it whether he likes it or not. Homework for a child is like a job is to an adult: a personal responsibility. Like the satisfaction an adult gets from a job well done, Thomas *will* feel better about himself if he does the work and his grades improve.

Doing homework is not his parents' responsibility—but they are responsible for providing the right environment and support. They should encourage Thomas without getting too involved in the day-to-day details. They should talk with him about his work, using the effective communication techniques we have talked about throughout this book.

Problem-Solving, Not Fault-Finding

Usually when parents and children have a problem, they end up getting mad and blaming each other. This is *problem-finding* behavior, and it leads nowhere. Instead, we advocate *problem-solving* behavior. That means, that instead of criticizing or nagging, you and the child sit and talk calmly, looking for a workable solution that satisfies both of you.

Your reaction may be, "How can a child possibly find solutions to his own problems?" You'd be surprised, if you let your child try, how many good ideas he might have. And in any case, if he does not agree with the solution, you'll never be able to enforce it against his will.

To solve a problem, you have to break it down into all its separate elements. Thomas has difficulties in the four main homework problem areas:

1. Remembering assignments
2. Starting homework
3. Completing the work
4. Checking the work

Thomas's homework solution will need to address these issues: he needs a system that will help him get the assignments home, and that will tell him when to start, where to work, and how long to work.

Remembering Assignments

The first problem that has to be solved is that Thomas forgets his assignments. Instead of writing them down in a single place, he writes them down on little scraps of paper, which tend to disappear. Without the assignments, nothing can be done.

We recommend a little notebook that he can keep in his

pocket. Besides writing down the assignment, he should also note all the materials he'll need, such as any textbooks. Then, at the end of the day, he can check over his list and make sure he's got everything he needs with him.

A Realistic Schedule

Now that he knows *what* the assignment is, the next questions are: How long will it take? When should it be done? And where should it be done?

How Much Time?

Thomas and his parents met with the teacher to find out how long he should be spending on his assignments every day—an hour to an hour and a half is typical in grade school and junior high.

What Time of Day?

The next step was for Thomas and his parents to decide what period of time, every day, will be set aside for homework. Notice that we said that Thomas *and* his parents should decide on a time. In order for this schedule to work, Thomas has to agree to it. He should feel like he is in control, so that he'll have a stake in making the schedule work.

Thomas chose to work from 4:30 to 6:00, so that he'd have an hour to play with his friends after school. His parents would have preferred that he did his homework first, but they agreed to give this schedule a trial.

Negotiating a Contract

We recommended that Thomas and his parents write up a homework "contract." This does not have to be an elaborate document; it can just be a simple checklist. But both you and your child have to agree to stick to it. This is what Thomas' homework contract looked like:

HOMEWORK CONTRACT

THOMAS AGREES TO:
1. Write down all assignments, review before leaving school
2. Start homework at 4:30 p.m.
3. Work until 6:00 p.m.
4. No breaks for TV, telephone, etc., until work is done

MOM AND DAD AGREE TO:
1. Enforce contract without nagging or yelling
2. Get a desk for Thomas's bedroom
3. Keep the house quiet while Thomas works (no loud TV)
4. Review Thomas's work and answer questions between 5:30 and 6:00 p.m.

As you can see, both sides have to offer something for a negotiation to work. Make sure the agreement is realistic, otherwise neither of you will be able to follow it.

Backsliding

There will be probably be days when Thomas forgets an assignment, or does not work during his scheduled time. But it won't help if his parents start nagging and criticizing. Thomas has made an agreement with them and himself. They should gently remind him of that and tell him that they trust him to do better next time.

They should give the contract they negotiated a trial for at least a month. If it's not working, then they can renegotiate it.

With their caring and nonjudgmental support, Thomas will learn that he can succeed and do well on his own. That success will motivate him to continue to work hard.

HOMEWORK HINTS

You may think that it's impossible to change your child's homework habits, but it's not. A very effective program for ensuring that homework gets done (and gets done *well*) is described in a book called *Winning the Homework War* by Dr. Fredric M. Levine and Dr. Kathleen M. Anesko. We can't review all of their suggestions, but here are a few of the recommendations they make.

Identify Specific Problems

Different homework problems need different solutions. Some children are disorganized, others have trouble concentrating, others simply aren't motivated or refuse to do the work. Homework hassles usually fall into one of five categories, although many children have problems in more than one area (see the following Homework Problem Category Checklist). To begin, you should concentrate on solving one or two specific behaviors that are the biggest problems. Again, don't demand perfection, just improvement.

HOMEWORK PROBLEM CATEGORY CHECKLIST

I. Doesn't Know What Homework to Do
- Isn't sure exactly what assignment is
- Forgets books or other materials at school
- Completes assignments, but leaves them at home or forgets to hand them in

II. Doesn't Know When to Do Homework
- Has to be reminded to start homework
- Procrastinates, puts off starting work
- Doesn't work well if alone in room
- Doesn't work well without help (from parents, older brother or sister)

III. Doesn't Know Where to Do Homework
- Doesn't work well if alone in room
- Doesn't work well without help (from parents, older brother or sister)
- Daydreams or plays with things during homework session
- Easily distracted
- Takes too long to complete homework

IV. Doesn't Know How to Do Homework
- Isn't sure exactly what assignment is
- Whines or complains about work
- Has to be reminded to start homework

- Procrastinates, puts off starting work
- Doesn't work well if alone in room
- Doesn't work well without help (from parents, older brother or sister)
- Easily frustrated by assignments
- Is dissatisfied, even if the work is done well

V. Doesn't Know Why Homework Should be Done

Defiant:

- Denies having assignments
- Refuses to do assignments
- Easily frustrated by assignments
- Responds poorly when told to correct work
- Deliberately fails to hand in completed assignments

Unmotivated:

- Fails to bring assignments and materials home
- Whines or complains about work
- Procrastinates, puts off starting work
- Produces messy or sloppy work
- Hurries through work, makes careless mistakes
- Forgets to bring assignment to class

Talk to the Teacher

The first step to take in dealing with your child's homework problems is to talk to the teacher. A couple of weeks into each term, you should touch base and find out what materials will be covered, what kinds of homework will be given, and how much time your child should spend on homework. This will give you a rational basis for determining if there is a homework problem and how to solve it.

After you have identified your child's problem, talk to the teacher to get his or her perspective. If you have questions about the kind or amount of work the teacher has assigned, talk to the teacher about your concerns.

Analyze the Home Atmosphere

Do you provide an atmosphere that promotes homework? We know parents who tell us their child is lazy or can't concentrate on his work, but who are as likely as not to interrupt the child when he's doing his work to have him babysit or do some other household chore. Does your child have a quiet place to work, free from distractions such as telephones, TV, and visitors? If not, it's no wonder he can't concentrate. It's up to you to make it clear that homework is important and valued by the whole family.

Make Enough (But Not Too Much) Time for Homework

The amount of time children are expected to spend on homework varies from school to school and grade to grade. Typically, younger children get less, while older children get more.

Unfortunately, there has been a trend lately to give less and less homework. In some schools, children get no formal homework until junior high school. This is unfortunate, because they are suddenly inundated with complex assignments, even though they never got any practice in developing their study skills.

Some educators recommend that the "ideal" study schedule is ten minutes a day times the child's grade level: that means ten minutes a day for a first-grader, and two hours a day for a high school senior.

Be a Homework Consultant, Not a Doer

If you're doing your child's homework, you're doing him more harm than good. You're teaching him that he does not have to do his own work—and even that he *can't*. If the work is really too hard for your child, get in touch with the teacher immediately to find out what's wrong.

Also, you should not get bogged down in the details of your child's homework, just the principles and process of it getting done. Part of the value of homework is it teaches the child to set his own limits and to discipline himself. The best way to help is to listen sympathetically, and not lecture. If your child asks for help, give support and guidance, but encourage him to find the answers and solve the problems for himself.

HOMEWORK HASSLES: QUIZ YOURSELF

When your child is having trouble with homework, your response can either help him solve the problem or compound it. Which of the following response would you most likely give if your fourth-grader complained that he had to do twenty multiplication problems that night?

1. That's not fair: I'll help you do them.
2. You're going to have to get used to tough assignments if you expect to get into a decent college.
3. That's nothing—when I was your age, I had twice as much work to do, and I was expected to help around the house, too, young man.
4. Your brother was in that same course two years ago and he never complained that it was too hard.
5. That's sounds like a lot of work; I bet it'll be really tough and tedious to get through.

The first four answers are all counterproductive. Number 1 suggests that homework assignments don't have to be taken seriously. Answers 2, 3, and 4 blame, criticize and put down the child, hurting his self-esteem.

But if you chose answer 5, congratulations! This response is both sympathetic and encouraging. It conveys the message that you understand that he will have to work hard, but that you expect him do it—and that you're confident he'll succeed.

In the next two chapters, we will discuss various strategies parents may use to get help. In Chapter Eight we focus on the strategies for interacting with the school system, while Chapter 9 is devoted to other avenues of assistance.

CHAPTER 8

SCHOOL STRATEGIES FOR GETTING HELP

NOWADAYS, PARENTS are taking a much more active and assertive role in their children's schooling than in the past. A generation ago, when parents went to school conferences, they would usually just sit and listen passively while the teachers and administration told them what decisions had been made about their child's schooling.

Those days are gone, for better or for worse. Today, parents have a right and a need to be more actively involved in their child's educational program. You should communicate with your child's teachers on a regular basis, understanding that you are partners in your child's educational welfare. If your child has any special problems or needs, you should explain them to each new teacher he encounters.

PARENTS' RIGHTS

The school cannot be expected to solve all your child's problems, or carry out your parental responsibilities. Still, you do have a right to ask for their cooperation in helping you cope with these problems. (Remember: You shouldn't complain if you haven't asked for the school's help, or all you do is criticize and blame the teacher!)

• The school should keep you informed about your

child's development. If trouble is brewing, you should be told right away, not at the end of the term.

- Homework loads should be regular, not erratic, so that you can help your child schedule his time effectively.
- The teacher should be willing to reassess your child's behavior and achievements; he or she may unconsciously assume the child is continuing previous poor behavior patterns even when the child has improved.
- Your child should not feel like he is being singled out, ridiculed, or otherwise discouraged by either the teacher or other students.

Special Education

If your child has a learning disability, ask about the school's special education program—your child may be eligible for help he's not getting. Regulations governing special education programs vary from state to state, but some basic rights are guaranteed under Federal Public Law 94-142, which defines special education as follows:

Specially designed instruction, at no cost to parents or guardians, to meet the unique needs of a handicapped child, including classroom instruction, instruction in physical education, home instruction, and instruction in hospitals and institutions.

Who Qualifies for Special Education?

A variety of educational handicaps can qualify a child for special education. These handicaps can range from learning disabilities to communication disorders, behavioral problems or mental retardation. Though there is some state-by-state variation, the commonly used classifications include learning disabled (LD), emotionally disturbed or emotionally handicapped (ED or EH), behaviorally disordered (BD), neurologically impaired (NI), mentally retarded (MR), and gifted (G). Special education is intended for children whose educational needs are quite different from those of their peers and who cannot learn effectively with regular educational methods and materials.

Whether your child qualifies depends on your state's special education code and how it defines specific educational disabilities. If you think your child is qualified but the school does not provide special education services, you can appeal the decision to the school board or the state department of education.

Tutoring and Remedial Programs

Even if your child does not qualify for a formal special education program, the teacher or school counselor may recommend remedial work or tutoring to help your child keep up or catch up with his grade-mates.

Giftedness

Exceptionally gifted students also have special educational needs, although the states have no obligation to provide special programs for them. Still, some schools do have programs that allow gifted children to develop academic, artistic or leadership skills. If your child is exceptionally bright, he may be bored by regular classes, which could lead to discipline and behavior problems. Find out if your school offers any special programs or classes. You may also want to ask about advanced placement and special outreach programs at local colleges and universities.

However, parents should realize that some children do extremely well academically *without* advance placement or special tracking programs. In fact, some educators believe that the process of labeling children impedes education, even for the exceptionally bright child. As one high school principal told us, "the more labeling, the less learning. Most teenagers dislike anything that separates them from their peers, so advance placement labels may actually do more harm than good." According to this theory, the best educational environment is a heterogeneous classroom, where children of different academic abilities are allowed to progress at their own rate.

College Preparation

Choosing a college may be the first major decision your child has ever had to make—a decision that may affect the rest of her life. Selecting the right college is seldom an easy task, and many children spend several months agonizing over their choice. And there is a great temptation for the parents to intercede on behalf of their favorite school. Of course a parent does have the right to voice their opinion, especially if they will be paying for their child's education. No school should be beyond the financial capabilities of the family (however, remember that many expensive schools offer very enticing financial aid packages). Nevertheless, financial considerations aside, selecting a college should be your child's responsibility. Avoid too much pressure to get into the "right" school. For most children there are a number of acceptable colleges. The following steps should help make the choice easier:

1. Talk to your child. If you haven't done it before, do it now. Ask your child what subjects he really likes, what possible careers he would like to pursue, and what colleges he has considered.

2. Talk to your child's guidance counselor. Ask him or her not only for an opinion of your child's strengths but also for recommendations on colleges. Many guidance counselors will have a wide selection of college catalogues available.

3. Visit prospective schools with your child. Whenever possible, talk informally to older students and professors regarding what their school is really like. Ask them about the intellectual and social environment, and—if financial aid is a factor—ask if the college has a reputation for drastically cutting financial aid for upperclassmen. (Some colleges have been reported to offer enticing financial aid packages to incoming first-year students, only to cut the aid tremendously in subsequent years.)

4. Collect information (brochures, videotapes, pamphlets) about prospective schools, as well as the independent books that review the different schools. Remember though that much of this information is "sales material," and may not give an accurate picture of a school. (One excellent but very northern college, managed not to include any pictures of snow in their photographs. Instead students were seen strolling over green campuses and lying at the beach of a nearby lake. In reality, "beach days" were reduced to one or two days a year, and students usually hurried across snow-covered campuses.)

5. Make certain that prospective schools are within the family's budget. One friend reports that she dearly regrets—

every month—the personal loans she incurred to go to the school of her dreams—loans that she is still paying off ten years later.

6. Apply to at least one "safety" school. Pick at least one acceptable school where your child should be admitted and examine the school's criteria for the most recent entering class (their SAT scores, high school grade averages, and geographical distribution). Make certain that your child will *comfortably* meet these criteria.
7. Remember that the final decision should be your child's.

WHAT SHOULD YOU DO IF...

Your child has problems with a specific teacher or class?

First, seek a special conference with the teacher—don't wait for him or her to contact you.

Parent-teacher conferences can be nerve-wracking. Many of us still are a little intimidated by schools and teachers, and we dread hearing about our children's academic and social problems. We also worry that if we are critical of the teacher, he or she may take it out on our child. *Do not let this keep you from your goals.*

Throughout this book, we have stressed the importance of approaching the teacher as an ally—not an enemy. Your goal should be to join him or her in helping your child. Dorothy Rich, in her excellent book, *Mega Skills* (Houghton Mifflin) suggests some specific tips to take the edge off your conferences and ensure a constructive outcome that will help your child.

1. Go into the conference with an open mind, prepared to listen to what the teacher has to say.
2. Set the tone by starting with some kind of positive (but truthful) statement about the teacher or the school. This could be something as simple as complimenting the artwork displayed in the classroom, as long as it's sincere.
3. Let the teacher know if there is any special stress on the child, such as divorce, an illness or death in the family, the birth of a new baby, or a move (see the Child Stress Symptoms, on p. 82). Understanding these pressures can

help the teacher communicate more effectively with your child.

4. Discuss general issues about your child, starting with his strengths—for example, special talents, skills, or hobbies. You should also discuss any special problems he has (like being overweight or a speech difficulty).

5. Next, talk about areas in which you think your child needs help: for example, that he needs to improve his study habits or control his temper better.

6. Ask about grades: How were they decided? How does your child compare with others in the class?

7. Find out what you can do to help the child at home.

8. Don't leave the conference with unanswered questions, and if you don't understand something the teacher said, ask him or her to explain it again.

9. Follow up on your conference. If there were areas needing improvement, make it your business to get back into touch with the teacher to see if progress is being made. Don't wait for the teacher to call you.

10. Remember that the teacher's evaluation—no matter how thoughtful—is only part of the picture. You see your child at home, and you should share this side of your child with the teacher.

If your child's problem with a specific teacher persists?

While most of your child's problems with a specific teacher can be resolved in a parent-teacher conference, occasionally a problem may persist. In this situation, the parent should contact the school's principal directly. The principal should be able to intervene and resolve the problem quickly, and if necessary arrange a rescheduling of your child's classes.

If your child has problems with school in general?

In high school, the first person to contact is your child's guidance counselor. In fact, guidance counselors have become so effective that many schools in the lower grades have added them to their staff.

Some schools without guidance counselors may use a "team teaching" approach. This approach is more common in the more structured environment of middle school, where students take the same courses and have the same teachers. In the team approach, teachers meet once a week to discuss their students and any problems they may be having. If your school has a team-teaching approach, you may find that discussing your child's problems with this team to be extremely helpful.

At the elementary level, a general school problem can be most effectively dealt with by the school's principal.

If your school's guidance counselors and/or principal cannot resolve the problem to your satisfaction, then your school district may provide the solution. Many school districts are now required by law to provide school psychologists.

Other school districts have established ombudsman or trouble-shooters to prevent problems from growing. Some school districts have created directors of instruction—these directors may be especially helpful in resolving problems with curriculum or educational practices.

If the school district does not have an ombudsman or director of instruction, a parent may contact the superintendent of schools, and even the school board itself if a serious problem has not been resolved.

If your child "flunks" a grade?

If your school suggests your child stay back a year, don't panic. Do not assume that your child is stupid, or that you have done a terrible job of parenting. Instead discuss the situation carefully with the teacher, guidance counselor or principal. Try to understand their reasons for wanting your child to stay back a year, as well as the cause or causes of your child's problems and the potential remedies. Remember that it is best for your child not to be struggling academically or socially, but that being left back may be very demoralizing. Understand too, that in the early years, boys tend to mature more slowly than girls. Therefore, the *youngest* boy in a class may benefit from being held back a year. For social reasons, we generally discourage children from either falling behind or advancing of kids their own age. Although high school students, because of academic difficulties, may need to take an extra year to develop their academic strengths.

If you are moving into a different school district?

Changing schools can be very disruptive and unsettling, no matter what the child's age. Younger children may find the new building and people intimidating, while older children may be more upset about leaving their friends. Furthermore, the child may find that the new school is more advanced in certain subjects, while behind in others, making the transition even more difficult.

Most people believe that the best time to move and switch schools is during the summer, before the new school year starts. However, some educators recommend that the *best time to move is during the school year.* According to these experts, the child entering a new school in February, for example, will have the spring to make friends and the summer to cement their new friendships. Without this opportunity, a new student may find the beginning of the school year even more intimidating and alienating, especially as they stand by and watch their new classmates revive old friendships.

To help new students adjust, some schools have adopted a "buddy system." In this system, a new student is paired with an established student, who has the responsibility of introducing the new student to classmates and of helping the child adjust to life in the new community.

The best way to deal with your child's fears and anxieties about moving are to acknowledge them, and to have patience.

Don't belittle your child's fears and anxieties with phrases like "you're too old for that whining," or "you'll make lots of friends at the new school," or "you'll forget all about your old friends soon enough." Instead, talk openly with your child about his fears and anxieties, and work together to find ways to address his fears. If he's worried about losing touch with old friends, you might suggest that he plan to write them regularly. But don't give him false assurances, and don't sweep his fears under the carpet.

How can a parent evaluate prospective schools in a given area?
For families moving into a new school district, *the best way to gather objective data about prospective schools is to consult a real estate agent.* Many real estate agencies collect up-to-date statistics concerning a school's average SAT scores, number of scholarship winners, percentage of students attending college, etc.

However, objective data such as the number of scholarship winners may be misleading. A high school with 1,600 students should have more scholarship winners than a high school with 500 students, and yet the smaller school may be the better school. And even a school with legitimate academic achievements may not practice an educational philosophy that you feel is appropriate.

Probably the best way to evaluate a school is for you and your child to visit the prospective school. Try to meet the teachers and the people in the administrative office, and find out as much as you can about the curriculum, after-school activities, clubs and community programs. Observe the school's environment, look at the walls and physical condition of the school: is the school proud of its students? Does the school's environment seem as if it would be conducive to a good education?

Another excellent way to gauge a school is by word of mouth. Talk to parents of children in the school or neighborhood. Try to find parents that share your values and concerns. Usually these parents are excellent sources of information, both good and bad, about a prospective school.

Getting this information can help your child feel more secure and oriented, and will help you select the best school for your child.

SPECIAL TIPS FOR SINGLE OR DIVORCED PARENTS

If you're married, your spouse is an important resource in helping you deal with your child's problems: when one of you simply can't cope, the other can take over. If you're a single parent—especially if you have a full-time job outside the home— you've got a double whammy. Still, you're not all alone: you can use the school as an additional resource.

First of all, do not hesitate to inform the school about your marital status—not so the child will be stigmatized, but so the teacher will be more sensitive. In addition, you can ask him or her to help monitor your child for any signs of adjustment problems. Also, make sure that copies of report cards and evaluations are sent to the other parent: even if you're divorced, you should both stay involved (and united) when it comes to your child's education.

You can use the school as a community resource center, whether you're divorced or not. The school may already host groups like Parents Without Partners; if it doesn't, consider organizing a parents' group on your own. It doesn't take much time or money to do: all you need is the school's permission to use its facilities, a mailing list of the school's single-parent families or space in the school newsletter to announce the club's formation, and dues to cover the administrative and custodial costs involved in providing school facilities.

Of course, you don't have to limit membership to single parents: it's just that singles are the ones with the fewest other support systems. The kinds of events you can plan are limited only by your membership's imagination and budget: activities could include potluck suppers, theater evenings, movie screenings or lecture programs in the school auditorium, or family sports outings, such as ice-skating, hiking, or beach parties.

In the next chapter we will discuss other avenues of help (psychiatrists, psychologists, and national resources) that a parent may wish to consult.

CHAPTER 9

HELP FROM OTHER SOURCES

COMMON SENSE, concern, and communication are the most important skills for helping your child with school problems. But sometimes even with the best of intentions, they're not enough. *Anytime you believe your child's problems are getting away from you, get help.*

Asking for help is not an admission of failure, or an indication that you are not a good parent. It shows that you care enough to give your child all the support he needs. When your child is having trouble, remember that you are not alone. Thousands of other parents have been where you are. We are all vulnerable to the same pain and unhappiness when our children have problems. When trouble strikes, reach out for help—to the school, to community groups, or to medical professionals.

You can also get help from the many excellent books on childhood development and learning problems that are available in bookstores and libraries. You'll find a selected list of some of these books at the end of this chapter. Learn as much as you can about your child's problems. After all, *you* are the ultimate expert on your own child.

GETTING PROFESSIONAL HELP

In Chapter One, we outlined the normal stages of childhood

and some of the typical difficulties children face. Most of the problems children experience are normal, and with your love and support, they adjust. But other times, you and your child need extra help. If your child has severe or persistent problems, or you suspect a learning disorder, the first thing you should do is take him to your family physician or pediatrician for a complete medical evaluation. He or she may recommend that your child also be evaluated by a psychologist or psychiatrist.

Picking a Doctor

If you don't have a doctor you see regularly, get one—even if there's nothing wrong with your child right now. In fact, many doctors like to do a "baseline" evaluation—that is, a check-up to determine what's normal (physically and emotionally) for your child. That makes it easier for him or her to diagnose and treat your child: when things go wrong, the doctor can use your child's normal condition for comparison.

One of the best ways to find a doctor is through recommendations from family and friends. You can also get the names of qualified physicians in your community from your local medical society or by contacting:

The American Medical Association
535 North Dearborn Street
Chicago, Illinois 60610 Telephone (312) 645-5000

Don't assume that just because your best friend likes a certain doctor, that he or she is the ideal doctor for your child. Be choosy when you pick a doctor; in addition to trusting in his or her professional expertise, you should be able to talk openly and have a good rapport with your child's physician.

Psychiatrists, Psychologists, and Counselors

Unfortunately, a number of people are embarrassed by the need to see a psychiatrist or psychologist. If your child broke his leg, you'd take him to an orthopedic surgeon, so why not take him to a psychiatrist when he's in emotional pain? The same goes for you—there's no shame in asking for psychological help so that you can give your child all the love and support he needs.

Your pediatrician or family doctor may be able to recommend a psychiatrist or psychologist. In addition, there are many community counseling services: the school, local hospital, or religious and community groups are all potential sources for referrals. If medication is being considered, remember that only a physician, such as a pediatrician or psychiatrist, can prescribe medication.

In some cases, a child specialist, such as a child psychiatrist, should be consulted. A child psychiatrist is a psychiatrist with special training in childhood disorders and treatment programs.

If alcohol and drug abuse is identified as a problem, there are many resources a parent can turn to for help. In addition to pediatricians, psychiatrists, and therapists, parents can seek out self-help recovery groups, such as Alcoholics Anonymous and Narcotics Anonymous. Often, a related program for families, such as Al-Anon and Nar-Anon, can be very helpful for parents wanting to learn more about the problems of addiction and of living with an addiction-prone family member.

Other Options

In addition to professional counseling, there are many organizations, self-help groups and school and community resources that can support you in dealing with your child's problems. The best place to start may be your school's Parent Teacher Association. Joining a support group allows you to network with other parents. Besides picking up valuable tips, insight and advice, it can be reassuring to know that you are not alone with your problems.

Protect Yourself

Although you should be open to advice and support from others, ignore or avoid people who make you feel guilty or put down because you can't "control" your child. Forgive yourself when you're overtired or overworked and you lose your temper or get involved in a senseless quarrel with your child.

When you feel down or overwhelmed, take a time out. Regain your perspective, and then get back to the business at hand:

doing your best to do what's in the best interests of your child.

NATIONAL RESOURCES

There are many organizations dedicated to children's development and education. The following is a list of a few national organizations that can provide helpful information to parents:

American Psychiatric Association
1400 K Street, NW
Washington, DC 20005

American Federation of Teachers
555 New Jersey Avenue, NW
Washington, DC 20001

Association for Childhood Education International
11141 Georgia Avenue, Suite 200
Wheaton, Maryland 20902

Association for Children and Adults
  with Learning Disabilities
4156 Library Road
Pittsburgh, Pennsylvania 15234

Association for Library Service to Children
c/o American Library Association
50 East Huron Street
Chicago, Illinois 60611

National PTA
700 North Rush Street
Chicago, Illinois 60611-2571

National School Boards Association
1680 Duke Street
Alexandria, Virginia 22314

Orton Dyslexia Society
724 York Road
Baltimore, Maryland 21204

Reading is Fundamental, Inc.
600 Maryland Avenue, SW
Suite 500
Smithsonian Institution
Washington, DC 20560

RECOMMENDED READING LIST

THERE ARE literally hundreds of books of advice on child care and education. Here are just a few that we think provide especially valuable insights into some of the common problems of school-age children. In addition, these books served as essential research resources in the preparation of this book. Most of these books were published recently and should be available in bookstores or your local public library.

Elkind, David. *The Hurried Child: Growing Up Too Fast, Too Soon.* Reading, Mass.: Addison-Wesley Publishing Company, 1983.

Faber, Adele, and Mazlish, E. *How to Talk So Kids Will Listen, and Listen So Kids Will Talk.* New York: Avon Books, 1980.

Frailberg, Selma H. *The Magic Years: Understanding and Handling the Problems of Early Childhood.* New York: Charles Scribner's Sons, 1959.

Ginott, Haim G. *Between Parent and Child: How to Get Through to Your Child.* New York: Avon Books, 1969.

Ginott, Haim G. *Between Parent and Teenager: How to Really Communicate with Your Teenager.* New York: Avon Books, 1971.

Ginott, Haim G. *Teacher and Child: Nurturing the Learning Child at Home and in Class.* New York: Avon Books, 1975.

Gordon, Thomas. *P.E.T. in Action: The No-Lose Way to Raise Happier, More Responsible, More Cooperative Children.* New York: Bantam Books, 1988.

Gordon, Thomas. *T.E.T.—Teacher Effectiveness Training: How Teachers Can Bring Out the Best in Their Students; How Parents Can Handle Their Children's Learning Problems.* New York: Peter H. Wyden, 1974.

Ingersoll, Barbara. *Your Hyperactive Child: A Parent's Guide to Coping with Attention Deficit Disorder.* New York: Doubleday, 1988.

Levine, Fredric M., and Anesko, Kathleen M. *Winning the Homework War: A Step-by-Step Method for Cultivating Good Homework Habits in Your Child and Defusing Homework Conflicts with Love.* Englewood Cliffs, NJ: Prentice Hall, 1987.

Levinson, Harold N. *Smart But Feeling Dumb: A Breakthrough Theory on the Diagnosis and Treatment of Dyslexia and How It May Help You and Your Child.* New York: Warner Books, 1984.

Meeks, John. *High Times/Low Times: The Many Faces of Adolescent Depression.* Summit, NJ: PIA Press, 1988.

Rich, Dorothy. *MegaSkills: How Families Can Help Children Succeed in School and Beyond.* Boston: Houghton Mifflin Company, 1988.

Shore, Kenneth. *The Special Education Handbook: How to Get the Best Education Possible for Your Learning Disabled Child.* New York: Warner Books, 1988.

Theroux, Phyllis. *Night Lights: Bedtime Stories for Parents in the Dark.* New York: Penguin Books, 1988.

Welsh, Patrick. *Tales Out of School: A Teacher's Candid Account from the Front Lines of the American High School Today.* New York: Penguin Books, 1987.

Weisberg, Lynne W., and Greenberg, Rosalie. *When Acting Out Isn't Acting.* Summit, NJ: PIA Press, 1988.

Saint-Exupery, Antoine de. *The Little Prince.* Orlando: Harcourt Brace Jovanovich

Adams, Paul; Berg, Leila; Berger, Nan; Duane, Michael; Neil, A.S., Ollendorff, Robert. *Children's Rights: Toward the Liberation of the Child.* New York: Praeger. 1971.

INDEX

About the Authors

DAVID A. GROSS, M.D. A well-respected, nationally-recognized clinician and teacher, Dr. Gross is the Medical Director of the Neurobehavioral Treatment Center and Clinical Director of Fair Oaks Hospital in Delray Beach, Florida. He has been published widely on the connection between neurology and psychiatry.

Dr. Gross is a magna cum laude psychology graduate of the University of Rochester. After a short stint as a grade school teacher in New York City, he attended medical school at the University of Florida, followed by completion of residency training in psychiatry at Yale University. Dr. Gross was the Chief Resident at Yale New Haven Hospital before joining Fair Oaks Hospital.

A board-certified psychologist, Dr. Gross specializes in problems of temper, anger, aggression and neurological disorders that can cause psychiatric symptoms.

IRL L. EXTEIN, M.D. Dr. Extein is the Medical Director and Director of the Neuropsychiatric Evaluation Unit at Fair Oaks Hospital in Delray Beach, Florida, and Psychiatrist-in-Chief at Lake Hospital of the Palm Beaches, Lake Worth, Florida. Dr. Extein is a Phi Beta Kappa graduate of the University of Chicago and received his medical degree from Yale University School of Medicine.

After completing his residency at Yale, Dr. Extein served as Clinical Associate at the National Institute of Mental Health before serving as Director of Neuropsychiatric Evaluation and Associate Director of Research at Fair Oaks Hospital in Summit, New Jersey. A psychopharmacologist, Dr. Extein specializes in the treatment of depression and drug dependency. His work has been widely published in the *American Journal of Psychiatry, Archives of General Psychiatry, Journal of the American Medical Association,* and other journals. He is the co-editor of *Guide to the New Medicines of the Mind* (PIA Press), and author of two American Psychiatric Association Press books.

SOLANO PARK
HOSPITAL
Designed for the Work of Life

2101 Courage Drive
Fairfield, California 94533

1-800-955-HOPE

SERVICES INFORMATION

Solano Park Hospital is a regional full service 80 bed inpatient psychiatric facility meeting the behavioral, emotional, and substance abuse treatment needs of children, adolescents, and adults.

Some of the problems Solano Park Hospital will treat include:
- Thought disorders
- Mood and behavior disorders
- Anxiety and panic disorders
- Stress disorders
- Substance abuse (adolescents and adults)
- Survivors of incest, trauma and other abuse

Some of the services Solano Park Hospital provides include:
- FREE Mobile Crisis Assessment Team
- A FREE 24-hour-a-day Crisis Assessment Service (to evaluate problems and make referrals to programs or professionals)
- Community education on mental health issues
- Partial hospitalization programs (day treatment)
- Specialized programs for children and adolescents with a fully accredited school for grades 1 thru 12
- Outreach centers located in Pinole and Napa

Solano Park Hospital provides the following programs:
- Adult Psychiatric
- Adult Dual Diagnosis
- Adolescent
- Adult ICU
- Child